MADE ON STATEN ISLAND

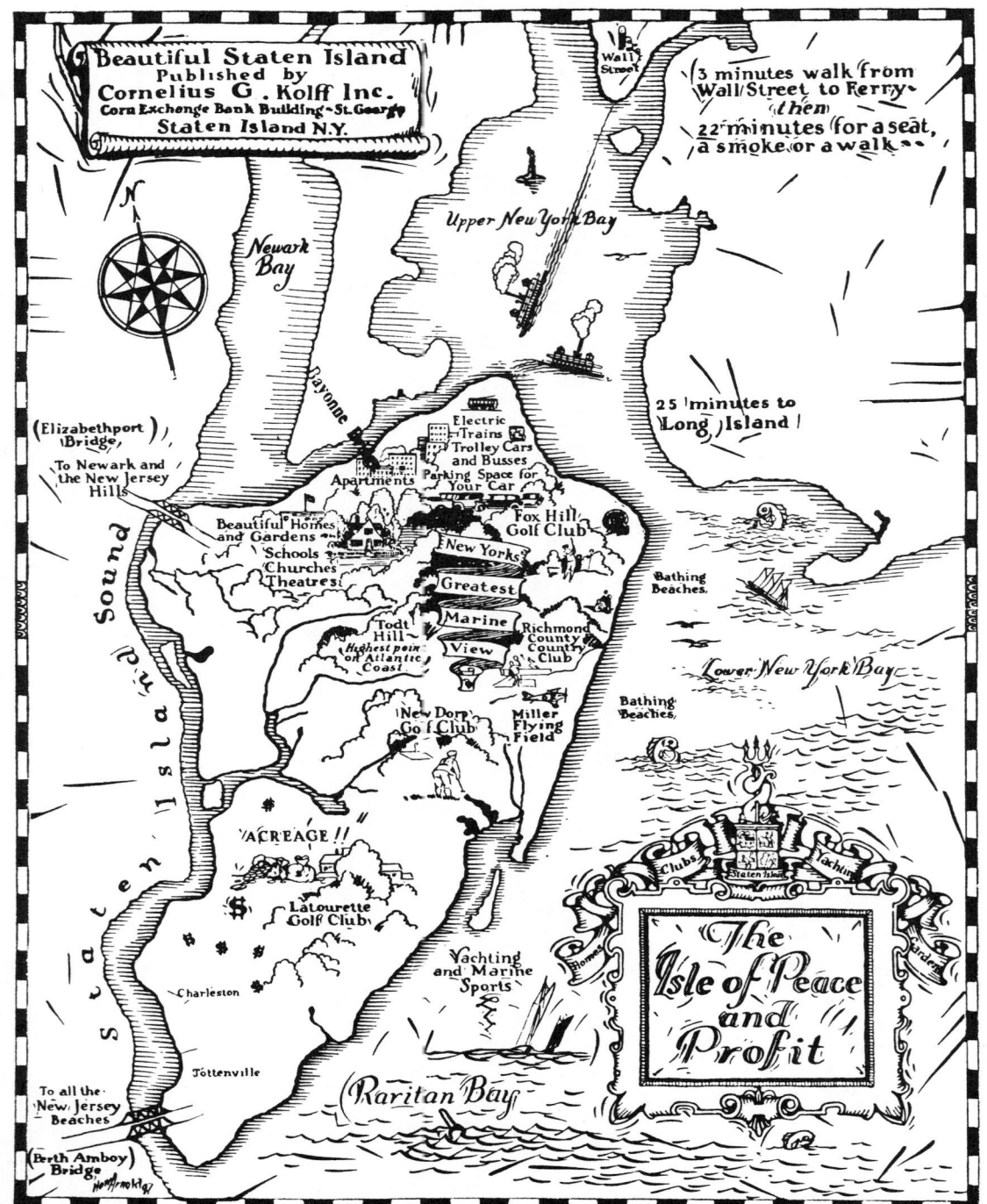

Made on Staten Island

AGRICULTURE, INDUSTRY, AND SUBURBAN LIVING IN THE CITY

by Charles L. Sachs

with the assistance of *Nancy H. Waters*

STATEN ISLAND HISTORICAL SOCIETY
Richmondtown, Staten Island, New York

Copyright © 1988 Staten Island Historical Society

Library of Congress Cataloging-in-Publication Data

Sachs, Charles L.
   Made on Staten Island.

   Bibliography: p. 114.
   Includes index.
   1. Staten Island (New York, N.Y.)—Economic conditions. 2. Staten Island (New York, N.Y.)—Industries. 3. Staten Island (New York, N.Y.)—Social conditions. I. Waters, Nancy H. II. Title.
HC108.N7S23   1988
330.9747'26043   88-24872
ISBN 0-9606756-0-4 (cloth)
ISBN 0-9606756-1-2 (paper)

COVERS:
Label from produce crate or can, Staten Island Preserving House, Long Neck (Travis), chromolithograph, ca. 1865.

FRONTISPIECE:
Flyer for "The Isle of Peace and Profit" published by developer Cornelius G. Kolff, 1927.

Made on Staten Island has been published in conjunction with the exhibition of the same title which opened at the Historical Museum, Richmondtown, in June 1984.

This publication has been made possible through the generous support of The J. M. Kaplan Fund and with the assistance of Westerleigh Savings, F.S.L.A., and the John Frederick Smith Publication Fund.

The exhibition was produced with the benefit of grants from the New York State Council on the Arts and The J. M. Kaplan Fund and additional contributions from the Staten Island Historical Society 1984 Museum Campaign.

The Staten Island Historical Society is an independent nonprofit cultural organization that manages Richmondtown Restoration for the city of New York. The city of New York owns the land and buildings of Richmondtown Restoration and supports part of its operations with public funds provided by the Department of Cultural Affairs. The society also receives support for its programs from the New York State Department of Education, the New York State Council on the Arts, corporations, foundations, and private individuals.

All objects and illustrations are from the collections of the Staten Island Historical Society unless otherwise credited. Acronyms used in the captions represent the following organizations: Museum of the City of New York (MCNY), New-York Historical Society (N-YHS), New York Public Library (NYPL), Staten Island Institute of Arts and Sciences (SIIAS).

CONTENTS

FOREWORD 7

ACKNOWLEDGMENTS 8

INTRODUCTION 11

PROLOGUE 15

THE RURAL ECONOMY 17
Mills 18   Farming 20   A Rural Craft 24
Alfred Cutting 25   James A. Morgan 26   The Oyster Industry 27
Seaboard Commerce 31   Maritime Trades 32   Shipyards 33

FACTORYVILLE 35
The Dyeworks Arrive 36   The Silk Printers 38
The Colonel's Factory 40   The Factory Village 42

MIDCENTURY GROWTH 45
The Breweries 46   Beer Gardens and Resorts 49
Soda, Seltzer, and Bottling Works 52   Cabinetmaking 53
Carriage Manufacturing 54   Louis Ettlinger & Sons 58
Louis Dejonge & Company 59   Clay Mines and Brick Works 60
Print-Cutting and Wallpaper Manufacture 64

INDUSTRIAL STATEN ISLAND 67

C. W. Hunt Company 68 *Every Branch of Industry* 70
Port Ivory 72 *The Factory by the Sea* 76 *Atlantic Terra Cotta* 80
Terra Cotta Design and Production 82 *Mayer's Confectionery* 86
Shipbuilding 88 *Linoleumville* 90 *Wild's for Wear* 94
Geza Nagyvathy 97

THE GREAT DEPRESSION 99

POLLUTION 101

PROHIBITION AND REPEAL 103

POST-DEPRESSION INDUSTRIES 105

ISLE OF PEACE AND PROFIT 109

SELECTED BIBLIOGRAPHY 114

INDEX 117

FOREWORD

The title of this volume and the exhibition it chronicles reflects the striking diversity of past economic activity on Staten Island. Throughout the nineteenth century and into the mid-twentieth century, Staten Island was the home to farming, heavy industry, and suburban living. Many present-day residents remember the truck farms along Richmond Avenue and Stapleton breweries, but few can recall the heavy industries like the Old Staten Island Dyeing Establishment and the C. W. Hunt Company in West New Brighton and the shipyards on our shoreline.

Made on Staten Island reminds us how quickly such economic diversity can vanish, for today's Staten Island is almost exclusively a suburban enclave, a bedroom community for the commercial and business centers of Manhattan. Our proximity to the great city center with its density, sophistication, and speed, exaggerates our rural quality. Although we are losing much of our open land and have already lost our farms, our island geography still allows us to enjoy some of the remoteness and aloofness that our nineteenth-century counterparts enjoyed.

The inauguration of the Made on Staten Island exhibition on June 10, 1984 marked the reopening of the Richmondtown Historical Museum. The society's exhibitions have traditionally focused on the people and domestic environments of the colonial period and early nineteenth century. Made on Staten Island emphasized more recent history, concentrating on the industrial development of the late nineteenth and early twentieth centuries.

With few industrial objects represented in our collections, curators Charles Sachs and Nancy Waters scoured the country for the remains of Staten Island's industrial past, and the local community responded enthusiastically to their appeals for information and artifacts. The curators and the exhibition designers have done a splendid job of integrating over 1,000 objects into the story of the island's economy.

Special thanks for underwriting the cost of this publication are due The J. M. Kaplan Fund and Westerleigh Savings, F.S.L.A. The Kaplan Fund was also one of the principal donors for the exhibition itself. We are proud to present this publication as a permanent record of the exhibition, which will take its story beyond the walls of the museum.

Barnett Shepherd, Executive Director

ACKNOWLEDGMENTS

This publication and the exhibition it accompanies could not have been produced without the assistance of a great many people. Had it not been for the farsighted, often avant-garde, research and preservation efforts of the many dedicated volunteers and staff members of the Staten Island Historical Society, who over the past fifty years worked to build the museum and archival collections, this project would not have been possible. To the scores of donors and contributors to the collection and research files the society shall always be grateful.

I am most indebted to Nancy H. Waters, the assistant project director and co-curator of the exhibition, who collaborated closely on nearly every aspect of the endeavor from the beginning and supervised design, fabrication, and installation. She also oversaw the selection and preparation of the artifacts and images displayed and was responsible for most of the research for and the drafting of object label copy. Without her dedication, thoughtfulness, and administrative skills, Made on Staten Island would never have been realized.

Initial research for Made on Staten Island, supported by an exhibition planning grant from the New York State Council on the Arts, was expertly conducted by consultant Elsa Gilbertson. The primary resource files prepared by Ms. Gilbertson served as the essential data base for the project as a whole and will remain invaluable aids to any future study concerned with commerce, industry, or agriculture on Staten Island. Much of the bibliography at the end of this volume is a result of Ms. Gilbertson's efforts.

All members of the society's curatorial department contributed to the development of this project. Librarian/archivist Stephen C. Barto provided especially valuable research assistance and helped identify and select materials from the society's collection of documents and paper ephemera. Mable MacDonald, curator of costumes, helped organize the collateral gallery display of locally-made and -worn clothing and assisted with object preparation and installation. Former and present registrars Martin Williams and Sarah McNeill coordinated the details of the loan arrangements, shipping, insurance, photography, and inventory control.

The entire staff of the society should be ackowledged for its support and cooperation throughout the course of the project. I particularly want to thank Barnett Shepherd, executive director of the society, for his encouragement and promotion of the publication effort.

Many individuals and institutions provided essential research aid and access to collections during project planning and development. I would especially like to thank the following for their generous help and cooperation: Eloise Beil, Kristine Hogan, and Hugh Powell, Staten Island Institute of Arts and Sciences; Barry Leo Delaney, formerly at the Staten Island Museum; Wendy Shadwell, New-York Historical Society; Ed Rider, Procter & Gamble Manufacturing Company Archives, Cincinnati, and Robert Davidson, formerly with the Procter & Gamble Manufacturing Company, Port Ivory; James Rossi, formerly at the High Rock Park Conservation Center; Steven H. Miller, formerly at the Museum of the City of New York; Jon M. Williams, Eleutherian Mills Historical Library; Joyce Royer, Mariners Museum, Newport News, Va.; Sandra Buchman, Chesapeake Bay Maritime Museum; David J. Bohaska, Calvert Marine Museum; Norman Brouwer, South Street Seaport Museum; Maria DaRocha and Edwin B. Faulkner, Sun Chemical Corporation, Pigments Division; Lydia Land, Pennwalt Corporation; John Saturniewicz, Nassau Recycle Corporation; Patricia Parente and W. C. Boyd, Greif Brothers Corporation, East Coast Division. Important materials and research data were also generously made available by the Library of Congress; Museum of American Textile History; National Museum of American History, Smithsonian Institution; New York City Planning Commission; New-York Historical Society; New York Public Library; New York State Archives; and the Port Authority of New York and New Jersey.

Other individuals who provided valuable information and assistance include: Clinton F. Allen; Robert Anderson; Richard Axt; Kimball Beasley; John Bieser; Constance Clason Campbell; Oscar T. Conner; the late Percy Decker; Roland Fountain and Miss Elizabeth Fountaine; Adrian Gagestyn; Frederick Fried; June Cole Gilbert; the late Frank Guether; William Guether; Audrey Hacker; Duncan Hay; Joseph Helmer; Edna Holden; Marjorie Johnson; Marjorie Kerr; Emily and Paula Mayer; Loring McMillen; Bruce Mohlenhoff; Richard Monnich; Mrs. Walter A. Mungeer (Anne Smith); the late Rudolph Z. Nagyvathy; Mr. & Mrs. Adolph Ostwald; William J. Rigby; Vera Sieger; Diane Jones Sliney; Susan Tunick; Joseph Walsh; and the late Oscar Weissglass.

Many individuals and organizations donated artifacts and documents and research materials for the exhibition: Albert Anderson; Mr. & Mrs. Alfred Anderson; Robert Anderson; Evelyn Boquist; Constance Clason Campbell; the late

Mrs. N. H. Donald; Brooke Elkan; Alan Elenson; Donald Erkman; Andrew Ferretti; William C. Gotthardt; Henry Graepel; Greif Brothers Corporation, East Coast Division; William Guether; Joseph Helmer; Edna Holden; Robert McAndrew; Mr. & Mrs. William McMillen; Bruce Mohlenhoff; the late Rudolph Z. Nagyvathy; Nassau Recycle Corporation; Procter & Gamble Manufacturing Company; William J. Rigby; Christopher Schreiber; Vera Sieger; Virginia Sloan; Sun Chemical Corporation, Pigments Division; Anthony Trombino; U.S. Gypsum; Claire Walsh; Mr. & Mrs. Joseph Walsh; Herman & Floretta Witzig; Harvey Zucker.

In addition to the items from the society's permanent holdings, the exhibition has featured loans from the following individuals, organizations, and institutions: Mr. & Mrs. Robert J. Bergren; John W. Bieser; George Burke; Constance Clason Campbell; Frank Dotti; Adrian Gagesteyn; Mr. & Mrs. Charles J. Geiss; June Cole Gilbert; Charles and Larena Greinsky; Estate of Frank Guether; Audrey Hacker; Mr. & Mrs. Joseph Helmer; Edith Holtermann; Tina Kaasmann-Dunn; Mr. & Mrs. William McMillen; Richard Monnich; Mrs. Walter A. Mungeer (Anne Smith); Museum of the City of New York; Muss Development Corporation; Mr. & Mrs. Adolph Ostwald; Philadelphia Museum of Art; Procter & Gamble Manufacturing Company; William J. Rigby; Rocky Hill Community Group; M. Scott; Vera Sieger; Staten Island Institute of Arts and Sciences—Archives & Library and Staten Island Museum; Sun Chemical Corporation, Pigments Division; Marie Sutter; William Vaccaro; Mr. & Mrs. Joseph Walsh; and Edward Wynn.

The exhibition installation was designed by Breslin/Mosseri Design with graphic design assistance by Abby Goldstein. Fabrication was performed by Museum Quality Pedestals, Inc. and Stan Reifel Associates. Special features of the installation were prepared by Drobney Robinson Design; Terry, Chassman & Associates, Inc.; H-Y Photo Services, Inc.; and Syd Silberman of Media Design, Inc. I also want to express my appreciation to V. Amessé for the principal studio photography and to Tom Shidemantle for the lab work for this publication. Additional photographic credit is due Anthony Lanza, George Roos, Marshall Norstein, and Malcolm Varon.

Above all, I would like to thank my family—Deborah, Sarah, and Adam—for their patience, support, and understanding.

INTRODUCTION

"Staten Island is embraced in the county of Richmond. Its area is put down in the report of its supervisors at 30,233 [acres]. The general surface is rocky and hilly. A portion of the south and west side is level, and where not too wet furnishes excellent farming land. Its proximity to New York will ensure it a surplus of the population of that city, and along the navigable water which surrounds it is springing manufactories that are becoming daily more important. Its value does not consist in the agricultural capacity of its soil, but in its peculiar adaptability for furnishing sites for manufacturing establishments; and its heights, overlooking the bay and city, furnishing building spots for the summer villas of the wealthy citizens of New York."

—Theodore C. Peters, *Report on the Agricultural and Other Resources of the State of New York* (Albany, 1864)

Thus, well over one hundred years ago, Staten Island was being perceived as an area in which significant—and potentially conflicting—economic and social developments were taking place with increasing frequency. This contrasts sharply with the perception widely-held among local residents today that, until very recently, the island was largely rural, basically autonomous, and nearly homogeneous in population.

Geography has conspired to provide the island with a peculiar sense of identity. Here is a substantial, self-contained land mass—more than two times the area of Manhattan—strategically located at the entrance of a great Atlantic port and commercial center. Physically closer to the coast of New Jersey than to any part of New York, the island has always been affiliated politically with its slightly more distant neighbor. As part of the province, state, and since 1898 the city of New York, Staten Island remains a geographically integral subdivision—both county and borough—within and at the southernmost extreme of the metropolis.

Due in large measure to the island's location, the total number of inhabitants and relative density of settlement have always been slight in comparison with the rest of New York City and much of the surrounding region. Staten Island's 1986 population—approximately 374,600—is considerably lower than Manhattan's resident total for 1850.

These same features raise interesting questions and provide exceptional opportunities for inquiry. Because of its convenient scale, population size, and well-defined boundaries as both a geographical and political entity, Staten Island provides a convenient focus for historical study of a long-settled, discrete community at the edge of the expanding city.

For more than half a century, the Staten Island Historical Society has been actively involved in the collection, preservation, and exhibition of documentary and artifactual materials relating to all aspects of the island's past, and in the research, study, field exploration, recording, and publication of its historical findings. In the early 1980s the planned renovation of the society's Historical Museum building provided the opportunity for a major review of collections and a reconsideration of interpretive goals. Staff research uncovered a wealth of resources associated with late nineteenth- and early twentieth-century island work and life-styles and a diversity of local enterprises. Especially impressive was an abundance of material relating to the prominent, but neglected, history of industrialization and manufacturing.

A 1982–83 grant award from the New York State Council on the Arts enabled the society to launch a more intensive research effort and refine the plans for the exhibition, the first major installation dealing with New York City manufacturing and industrial history to be presented by a city cultural institution. The renovation of the Historical Museum building—nearly fifty years after it was initially adapted for museum purposes by the society and the WPA—provided the society with a renewed, modern facility in which to present interpretive historical exhibitions in a gallery setting, highlight portions of the society's extensive holdings, and supplement the installations and activities elsewhere in the Richmondtown Restoration complex.

Opened in June 1984, the inaugural exhibition, Made on Staten Island: Agriculture, Industry, and Suburban Living in the City (1800–1984), was designed to suggest the variety, complexity, and vitality of the island's contributions to the economy and culture of the metropolitan region. The installation, which occupies approximately 8,000 square feet of gallery space, utilizes more than 1,000 artifacts, images, and documents, as well as a video production of rare historic motion pictures, to trace the growth, transformation, and decline of local agriculture and industry, the impact of Staten Island's resources on the surrounding region, and the effects of urban and suburban growth on the borough's recent development. A broad assortment of objects and materials crafted, manufactured, and used on Staten Island between the late 1700s and the mid-1980s is included in the display, which has been designed and installed to complement and work within the distinctive interior spaces of the Historical Museum.

Given the material density and highly specialized nature of the installation, it would not have been practical to attempt to reproduce the exhibit in its entirety as a catalogue. Instead, we have adapted the material into a slightly different format. This publication presents all of the principal section essays from the exhibit (with minor revisions) and incorporates a representative selection of more than one hundred artifacts and images, the majority of which are published here for the first time. The text, like the exhibit, is divided into six major thematic chronological sections. Each of these contains one or more short chapters devoted to a particular industry or enterprise, or highlighting a noteworthy individual. The main focus of the work is the critical period of industrial development, transformation of traditional agribusiness, and the capitalization and decline of the shellfisheries that occurred between 1819 and 1930. A brief prologue examining the preindustrial economy and the work and life-styles of the late eighteenth and early nineteenth centuries, introduces the main body of the book. A more extensive epilogue, dealing with post-Depression and contemporary developments, serves as the conclusion. A bibliography of selected sources is appended to this volume as a guide to further research and study.

It is hoped that by examining the objects and materials used, crafted, manufactured, or otherwise produced on Staten Island between the late eighteenth century and the 1980s we have been able to explore changing patterns of land use, work, ethnicity, daily life-style, and overall economic development and discover the roots of many contemporary issues.

Charles L. Sachs, Chief Curator

PROLOGUE
The Turn of the Nineteenth Century

The birthplace of the late Rev. G. T. Bedell, formerly the Rose and Crown Tavern, Richmond Road and New Dorp Lane, New Dorp; steel engraving by H. Jorden after painting by James Smillie, from The Religious Souvenir for MDCCCXL *(New York, 1839).*

The last years of the 1700s and the first decade of the new century were times of quiet readjustment for Staten Islanders. Having survived more than seven years of military rule and occupation by as many as 30,000 British and Hessian troops, the small Staten Island population (3,835 in 1790—comprised of English, Dutch, and French immigrants; their frequently intermarried descendants; and 819 black slaves) began the tasks of restoring, rebuilding, and re-planting what had been damaged or destroyed during the Revolution.

Several of the island's wealthiest and most influential citizens, who had remained prominent Loyalists, fled to Canada after the war; their estates, confiscated by the state of New York, were subdivided and sold. As these large landholdings were broken up and the new state and county governments established authority with little difficulty, Staten Islanders returned to the traditional occupations and pursuits of the settlement prior to the Revolution.

Between 1790 and 1810 the island remained a predominantly rural area with an economy and culture founded on the principal occupations of farming, fishing, and maritime commerce. The population grew steadily, increasing more than 39 percent to a total of 5,347 by 1810. Although separated by water from the surrounding region, islanders remained closely associated with the neighboring New Jersey counties, western Long Island, and Manhattan, through family and business connections. In 1810 the main Staten Island industries were two textile carding machines, two tanneries, three distilleries, and fifty-nine looms in domestic use—producing 23,100 yards of flaxen goods, 7,000 yards of blended cloth, and 2,000 yards of woolen fabric for home consumption. At the turn of the nineteenth century, slavery was gradually ending in New York State. The steam engine, the suburb, and the factory had yet to arrive.

THE RURAL ECONOMY

A Brisk Gale in the Bay off Staten Island, W. J. Bennett, color aquatint, 1836. MCNY.

Despite developments in commerce, real estate, and industry, Staten Island retained much of its rural character throughout the nineteenth century. Well past the Civil War, large numbers of residents continued to make their livelihood and take their sustenance from the two most obvious resources—the land and the surrounding sea. The phenomenal urban growth of nearby Manhattan and Brooklyn helped preserve the agrarian identity of Staten Island by providing huge, ready markets for the products of farms and fisheries, and by creating a sharper contrast between the city and Staten Island's natural attractions.

"We had a fine drive through the most interesting parts of the island, the surface of which is much varied," the British traveler James Stuart wrote of Staten Island in 1829. "We saw many comfortable-looking farm houses amidst rich valleys and lands, and orchards abounding in fruit; but what most surprised me in looking at the fruit, was the extraordinary quantity of cherry trees producing the small black and red cherry."

"The whole island is like a garden, and affords very fine scenery," wrote Henry David Thoreau during a visit to the home of Judge William Emerson on Emerson Hill, Concord in 1843. In 1840 one-sixth of the Staten Island male population was engaged in agriculture, and nearly as many men were occupied in maritime pursuits—fishing and shellfish cultivation, shipping and navigation, boat construction and repair. As late as 1880 more than 44 percent of the area was still being used for agriculture (342 individual farms averaging forty-eight acres in size), and at least two hundred families depended on the oyster business for their entire support. Despite major technological advances and the widespread availability of inexpensive manufactured and imported goods from Manhattan and other nearby urban market centers, many handcraft traditions associated with rural life persisted well into the twentieth century.

MILLS

Buildings designed and fitted with machinery to harness natural energy for the refining of raw materials into more convenient or marketable forms had been constructed on Staten Island since the 1670s. At least twenty mills are known to have existed, powered either by the movement of fresh water from streams and ponds or the controlled flow of the tides.

Throughout the nineteenth century mills provided needed services to Staten Island farmers and tradespeople—grinding grain into flour, sawing timber to boards, carding wool, and aiding in other simple manufacturing processes. Despite continued active use, by midcentury these large rural factories were viewed by many city dwellers only as picturesque, romantic symbols of an idealized country life.

The massive tidal gristmill at the head of the Fresh Kill near Richmond was probably built about 1760. Known during the Revolution as Beadle's Mill, it was owned by a family named Crocheron from about 1800 to the early 1850s, when it was acquired by William Geib. Two Seaver brothers, Patrick and Lawrence, recent emigrants from Ireland, operated the mill for Geib from the early 1850s through the 1870s, when the building was sold to Simonsons. The structure remained in use to the end of the century; it was destroyed in 1922.

In the 1830s the first of a series of mills for the production of metal tools and equipment was established on the Willowbrook, on or near the site of the eighteenth-century sawmill owned by Nicholas Haughwout. Just above Joseph Hall's gun and, later, hardware factory, Thomas Standring built a second mill shortly after arriving from England in the mid-1840s. Here, Standring manufactured steel combs for use in the wool and cotton industries. In 1865 Standring's water-powered mill, operated by four full-time adult male employees, was producing $3,000-worth of combs from $500 of raw steel plate annually.

In the mid-1880s a gasoline engine was installed in the two-story wood frame building, replacing the overshot water wheel with a more efficient source of power. When Standring died in the 1890s, his son Samuel continued the operations, adding the manufacture of animal currying combs to the business. Samuel ran the mill until two years before his own death in 1922, after which time the building fell into ruin.

Thomas Standring in front of his comb mill on the Willowbrook, ca. 1885.

Old Mill at Richmond, C. Winter, oil on canvas, 1850. SIIAS. C. Winter, an American painter active in the 1850s, evokes more of a romantic fantasy scene than a realistic depiction of the reputed subject—Geib's (or the Seavers') Tide Mill at Richmond. This painting stands in marked contrast with Winter's other known Staten Island canvas, his detailed rendering of Richmond Village painted the following year.

Geib's Tide Mill (Richmond Mills), Richmond Creek and the foot of Old Mill Road, Richmondtown, ca. 1900.

FARMING

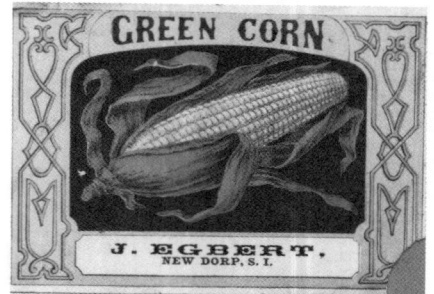

Produce can label, J. Egbert Farm and Cannery, New Dorp, 1868.

A Staten Island Farm Scene, engraving from Richard Edwards (ed.), A Descriptive Review of the Manufacturing and Mercantile Industries of the City of Brooklyn, and Towns of Long Island and Staten Island, 1883. SIIAS.

Because of its small size, its rocky, hilly, and sandy surface, and its long history of land cultivation, Staten Island was not an easy place to maintain an agricultural existence. The soil required continuous fertilizing. With the opening in 1825 of the Erie Canal, it became increasingly difficult to compete with the influx of cheaper wheat from the richer lands farther west. The island's greatest advantage for farming, however, was its "readiness of access to the best point of immediate consumption in the country."

At the beginning of the nineteenth century individual farm plots resembled those of the late colonial era. Averaging about eighty acres, roughly rectangular in shape, they often extended to the shore or ran along an inland waterway. Oxen were used to perform the heaviest farm work. Indian corn, wheat, potatoes, rye, barley, buckwheat, turnips, and flax were grown; horses and mules were kept for draft and the road; swine, cattle, sheep, and poultry were for food and market. The principal, most profitable crop throughout the century was hay, both the cultivated or "fresh" variety and the abundant, wild salt marsh grass, which was harvested for use and sale as animal feed, and was shipped by barge for the horses in the city.

By 1850 agriculture on Staten Island was undergoing subtle but substantial changes. Increased population and the development by wealthy New Yorkers of resorts, institutions, and suburban residences on the north and east shores had raised the price of land and had begun to restrict the areas available for farming.

Mille Farm, Staten Island, John Bradley, oil on canvas, 1835. SIIAS. This detailed primitive genre landscape is the earliest known image of a Staten Island farm scene and the only documented landscape by Bradley. Born in Great Britain, Bradley was active on Staten Island and in New York City from 1832 to 1847 and is best remembered as a painter of folk portraits. Among the first paintings Bradley made in America after emigrating from Great Britain were a series of at least ten portraits of the members of wealthy farming, merchant, and seafaring families from Westfield (the southernmost section of Staten Island) dating between 1832 and 1834. According to oral tradition, this painting depicts Andrew Mille's farmstead, which overlooked Prince's Bay (now included in Wolfe's Pond Park). The house is typical of the pre-Revolutionary War rural residences constructed along Staten Island's shores and throughout the lower Hudson River Valley.

In 1829 Andre or Andrew Mille (ca. 1780–1868), a "gentleman" from New Jersey, purchased a 132-acre tract of farmland— with its colonial farmhouse and outbuildings—located between Amboy Road and the beach at Prince's Bay for the sum of $4,500. Mille owned and occupied this property until 1838 when he sold it to Andrew Hood of New York City and moved to a 36-acre plot further inland in the Woodrow area.

Mille's farmstead later became part of Joel Wolf's holdings, part of which was sold in 1857 to New York state for use as a "temporary quarantine station" for suspected disease-stricken immigrants, ship passengers, and sailors entering the port. In May 1857 when protest went unheeded, "Wolf's farmhouse" and several other structures were burned to the ground by irate island citizens opposed to the plan.

THE RURAL ECONOMY

Rossville farmers with load of hay on oxcart, photograph by F. M. Simonson, ca. 1906. SIIAS.

Produce can label, David J. Tysen's Farm and Cannery, New Dorp-Oakwood, ca. 1870.

Diploma awarded to Thomas Sampson by the Richmond County Agricultural Society for the best four-year-old mare, September 29, 1866. Engraved and printed by William C. Robertson, New York City.

Staten Island farmyard scene, probably Decker family, Northfield (Bull's Head or New Springville areas), tintype (ferrotype) ca. 1870.

Among the "forners from New York" and newcomers from other areas who began settling on the island in the 1830s were a number of men of advanced education and scientific interest who sought the life of the "gentleman farmer." Buying large tracts of farmland along the island's more fertile south shore, these "book farmers" experimented with agricultural methods to make more efficient and economical use of the land and to increase production of better, more profitable crops. To share the results of their experiments and offer advice to their neighbors they founded a county chapter of the state agricultural society, held cattle shows and fairs, and corresponded with other "scientific" farmers across the country.

The 212 farms in existence at midcentury ranged in size from a fraction of one acre to three hundred acres—the average being less than fifty acres. The production of wheat and other cereals was decreasing. Hay remained the major crop, but the "truck business," market gardening, berry and orchard culture, and dairying for both city and suburban consumption, had gained considerable importance—as did the associated industries of canning, preserving, and packing and fertilizer processing.

THE RURAL ECONOMY

A RURAL CRAFT

White oak splint work baskets made by Alfred Cutting ca. 1880.

Oyster basket, oyster basket handles, market basket, and covered "fancy" basket, attributed to James A. Morgan, 1855–1910. According to family tradition, the unusual twill weave basket of white oak and maple splint dyed various colors (right) was one of the last produced by James Morgan of New Springville. It is unlike any other surviving example of his work—simply-plaited, utilitarian containers of carved white oak.

The making of baskets—simple containers of interwoven plant materials—was one of many traditional handcrafts commonly practiced by rural Staten Islanders. Due to the island ecology as a transitional area between northern ash and southern oak woodlands, with an abundance of swamp and wetlands, baskets of all three material traditions (oak and ash splint and cultivated willow) were produced here.

Even before the period of colonial settlement, Staten Island brown ash or "basket wood" was an important source of weaving material for the Native American inhabitants of the New York–New Jersey region. As late as the 1850s a few islanders of Indian descent were still known to be making baskets from pounded ash splint.

Before midcentury, basketry was predominantly a part-time domestic activity. Most farmers and watermen prepared their own hardwood splint and wove as many simple plaited vessels as they needed during the cold, rainy days or evenings of the winter and off-season. Ash was used for smaller work, especially berry and "fancy" baskets; sturdier containers were made of oak.

Willow work, however, was a highly specialized, skilled craft, requiring a lengthy apprenticeship to master the tools and techniques of production as well as the methods of osier propagation. Two English brothers, John and Sampson Read, settled on the island in the late 1810s and established basket-making businesses and plantations for willow cultivation that were continued by family members and apprentices for three generations. Other willow basketmakers from Germany, Poland, and France emigrated to the island just before and after the Civil War.

By the 1870s, when cheap, imported containers were readily available from New York City markets and a steam-powered basket and crate factory was operating in Rossville, local farmers and craftsmen were still making baskets by hand.

ALFRED CUTTING
Farmer, Laborer, Basketmaker (1820 – 1910)

From the 1860s through the 1880s, Alfred Cutting made and mended simple, plaited white oak splint baskets for his family's use at home and on their small farm. Basketry was just one of the many necessary craft activities—shoe, clothing, tool, and house repair; coopering; carpentry; butchering; broom making; and chair caning—performed during the months of December through March. He was never known as a craftsman; like other farmers, he just made the three to ten baskets he needed each year and taught his methods to his sons.

The youngest of eight children of Robert and Anna Cutting of Suffolk, England, Alfred Cutting emigrated to the United States with his family in 1823. The Cuttings settled in Brooklyn, where they established themselves as farmers, first in the Williamsburg section, and then in New Utrecht. Following Robert Cutting's death in the cholera epidemic of 1832, a number of the older children began to resettle in the Rossville area of Staten Island.

Alfred Cutting moved to Staten Island in the 1840s, where he made his living as a laborer and small-scale farmer. He married an English-born woman from New Jersey in 1854, and together they raised five children, living at first on small rented farm properties in the Rossville-Woodrow area. He supplemented the income from his vegetable and berry plots by helping on neighbors' farms, clearing woodlands, harvesting salt hay, and laboring in the nearby clay pits and J. D. Winant's basket factory.

In 1873 Cutting was finally able to purchase land of his own, a four-acre parcel on Sharrott's Road in Woodrow, on which he built a family homestead. He expanded his holdings and continued to farm with the help of his sons well into his old age.

Cutting's journal-account books provide a unique record of the daily life routines of rural Staten Islanders at the end the nineteenth century.

Alfred Cutting and members of his family in front of their home, 68 Sharrotts Road, Woodrow, ca. 1900–1910.

JAMES A. MORGAN
Oyster Basketmaker (1832–1915)

James A. Morgan, his wife, daughter, and grandsons in front of the Morgan house, Old Dock Road (opposite the intersection of Richmond Hill Road and Richmond Avenue), New Springville; photograph by McGregory & Martin, ca. 1892. Courtesy of Percy Decker, Sr.

The development of oystering as a major economic endeavor created by midcentury a need for large numbers of sturdy oak splint baskets as standard units of measure, transport, and exchange in the shellfish trade. Since this demand could not simply be met by the off-season production of island watermen, a new occupation arose—that of the full-time oyster basketmaker.

James A. Morgan was trained in and made his principal business the manufacture of oak splint oyster baskets. Born in New Springville, a descendant of an old island family of Welsh extraction, Morgan chose not to follow the occupations of his father—shoemaking, or his grandfathers—farming. Instead, he left school at age twelve to apprentice with an oyster merchant, Henry Miller, and learned the trade of basketmaking. Both his father and paternal grandfather had made or mended baskets on occasion for additional cash, but neither had thought of devoting themselves to the occupation full-time.

In the mid-1850s, James Morgan built a basket workshop behind his parents' house along the salt meadow of their one-acre farm in New Springville. After his father's death, James remained in the house, where he and his wife raised five children and looked after his widowed mother.

Morgan operated his basket shop for more than fifty years, producing handmade oak and maple splint baskets on molds for domestic as well as commercial use. In addition to market and oyster baskets, at the end of the century he made woven splint storage bins and shipping containers for the linoleum factory in Travis and the general stores in New Springville. As island wood grew scarce, he had logs shipped from New Jersey. He continued making baskets for sale until just before he died.

In the 1940s Morgan's son William constructed detailed wooden models of his father's house and shop and other local sites to help preserve a record of the island's rural past.

THE OYSTER INDUSTRY

Oysters had been gathered for food in the waters around Staten Island long before the arrival of European explorers. In the seventeenth and eighteenth centuries Dutch and English colonists enjoyed harvesting the natural shellfish bounty of New York harbor, the Hudson River, Kill Van Kull, Arthur Kill (also known as Staten Island Sound), and Prince's and Raritan Bays.

In spite of colonial and state laws that limited the oyster-gathering season and restricted access to local waters, most of the natural beds around Staten Island had been nearly exhausted from overfishing by the 1810s.

To preserve their livelihood and meet the increasing demand for this immensely popular American food, Staten Island and New Jersey watermen began to gather, import, and transplant the small "seed" or tiny, larval "set" oyster from fertile natural beds of neighboring communities and from the Virginia coast. By the 1840s, Staten Island oystering had been transformed from a dwindling extractive pursuit to a sophisticated form of underwater cultivation and an extensive trade in which substantial fortunes were made.

Oyster cultivation was labor-intensive. Added to the heavy physical work of the extractive fishery—raking and tonging the sea bottom with long wooden-handled iron tools, then culling, hauling, and shucking—were staking out, preparing and repeatedly cleaning the planting grounds; casting the "seed" oysters (750 bushels per acre); and periodically transplanting young shellfish to deeper beds.

"A number of large schooners are employed in the oyster trade between Staten-Island and Virginia," wrote Dr. Samuel Akerly in his report on island agriculture in 1842, "while smaller vessels ply between the oyster beds and the New-York market, to dispose of the fruits of the labor of a numerous class of men engaged in the business." By the early 1850s the oyster trade had become such a significant part of Staten Island and New York City economy and social life that it was universally considered to be one of the region's foremost industries. At least a thousand men were directly employed cultivating oysters around New York Bay at midcentury, when the trade began to grow more specialized in its operations and became dominated by large commercial firms.

By the 1870s, wealthy Staten Island planters, shippers, wholesale dealers, and commission merchants were furnishing oysters (opened and in the shell) as far west as the Rocky Mountains, supplying seed oysters to the Pacific coast, and

John I. Merrill Oyster Barge, foot of West 10th Street, New York City, ca. 1880. Courtesy of R. W. Monnich.

Abraham Martineau's oyster sloop, ferrotype (tintype), ca. 1870–80. Courtesy of Marjorie Johnson.

Edward Hesse Oyster & Lunch Room, Stapleton, photograph by George Bear, 1898.

Tonging oysters in Rossville Bay, the Arthur Kill, ca. 1900. SIIAS.

Oyster boats of Mr. Mersereau (left) and Ellsworth Lewis (right) in Raritan Bay, postcard, 1906.

"Oyster Row"—West Street (looking north from Charles Street), New York City, ca. 1890. MCNY.

exporting oysters to foreign countries. The headquarters of the industry were the floating barges and scows of Manhattan's "Oyster Row," which shifted location between the East and Hudson Rivers during the course of the century. As the industry grew, common-law traditions for claiming oyster beds were replaced by a formal legal system for deeding and renting underwater real estate. At the end of the century more than 200,000 bushels of oysters were still produced annually from Staten Island waters, but most small-scale, independent watermen had become the employees of the major planter-dealers.

Oystering at Prince's Bay, *Alex Matthew, oil on canvas, ca. 1853.* Nothing is known about the life of Alex Matthew, the naive artist who produced this version of a popular wood engraving published in several American illustrated periodicals during the 1850s. The painting depicts local watermen working on a Staten Island skiff, tonging for oysters in Prince's Bay. Crude poles mark the boundaries of individual oyster plots. The Red Bank Light can be seen on the shore.

Originally developed by local watermen for tonging oysters in the bays and inlets of Staten Island and northern New Jersey, the distinctive Staten Island or "Yankee" skiff was brought to the lower York River of Virginia by Staten Island and Manhattan oyster planters seeking more productive tonging grounds in the late nineteenth century. According to tradition, a Staten Island oyster packer, Peter Van Name, settled on the York River in the 1870s and popularized these skiffs among the many packing houses that rented them to local oyster tongers. By the early 1960s none of these boats were known to exist on Staten Island or the nearby New Jersey coast.

Illustration from "The Oyster Business," Ballou's Pictorial Drawing-Room Companion, *September 29, 1855.* Illustrated feature articles on the New York and Staten Island oyster industry appeared in a number of popular American magazines in the 1850s. Identical wood engravings with slightly different texts were printed two years earlier in the Illustrated News, *July 16, 1853.* The image inspired Alex Matthew's oil painting Oystering at Prince's Bay.

SEABOARD COMMERCE

Situated at the entrance of New York harbor and surrounded by bodies of water of considerable width, Staten Island has traditionally depended on the strength of its shipping connections for much of its economic well-being. Island-based mariners, sea captains, harbor pilots, ferry operators, and shipping merchants were important figures in and around the thriving nineteenth-century port of New York.

Captain Isaac Cole, whose heroic likeness was captured by an anonymous portraitist, is representative of a large group of successful contemporaries. Born near Richmond Valley in 1808, a descendant of a colonial island family many of whose members were seafarers, Isaac Cole owned and operated a fleet of schooners in the coastwise trade. He traveled regularly between Staten Island and the South, where some of his brothers and other relatives had settled, and reputedly carried Samuel F. B. Morse's telegraph wire for the first line between Baltimore and Washington. After losing a number of vessels during the Civil War, Cole retired from the sea in 1866, spending the rest of his life with his family in their majestically pillared Greek Revival home on Woodrow Road, farming their small plot of land and operating a grocery business. He died at age ninety-six, in 1904.

Capt. Isaac Cole (1808–1904), oil on canvas, ca. 1840. According to family tradition, this portrait was painted by an itinerant artist and presented to the sitter as a gift during one of Captain Cole's commercial visits to the South. The scene in the background is said to depict part of the captain's fleet of schooners entering the Narrows. The subject's left hand is resting on a copy of Nathaniel Bowditch's Navigator.

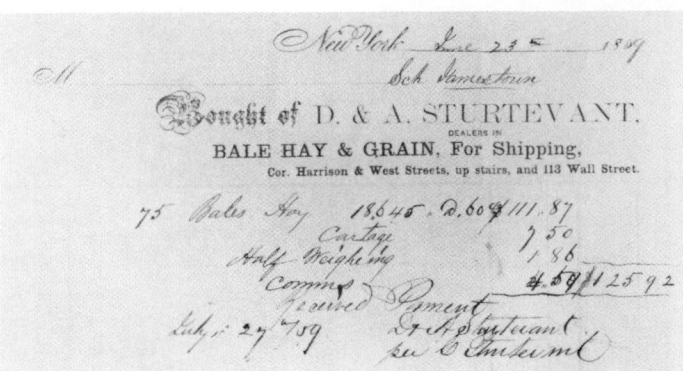

Receipt for seventy-five bales of hay purchased from D. & A. Sturtevant, June 23, 1859, which were loaded on Captain Cole's schooner Jamestown.

THE RURAL ECONOMY

MARITIME TRADES

Ross Sail Loft, Richmond Terrace, Port Richmond, ca. 1890.

Staten Island Whaling Company stock certificate for one share issued to Paul J. Mersereau, February 27, 1839 for fifty dollars.

The accessibility and potential richness of thirty-five miles of shorefront led many nineteenth-century Staten Island residents to "abandon the plow to go 'plow the deep,'" as one progressive farmer complained in 1842. "The domestic fishery too," he observed, "abstracts greatly from attention which would otherwise be applied to the cultivation of the soil."

During the months of March through May, part-time farmers and commercial fishermen set up large seines, drawnets and fikes along the southern and eastern shores to catch the schools of shad migrating south to the Gulf of Mexico. In June the mossbunker, a bony variety of herring, was netted for use primarily as a fertilizer. In the spring and fall blackfish, striped bass, weakfish, flounder, and other food fishes were hooked in deeper waters. Eels were speared or trapped along the shores and clams were dug with a hoe or rake on the beaches at low tide.

In support of the fisheries and shipping interests a variety of other trades and services arose. Sail lofts, which later also manufactured building awnings, were established on the north shore before midcentury; and rope walks were founded in Rossville and Richmond in the late 1850s. For the brief period between 1838 and 1842 the Staten Island Whaling Company operated the bark *White Oak* and a whale oil processing plant in Port Richmond.

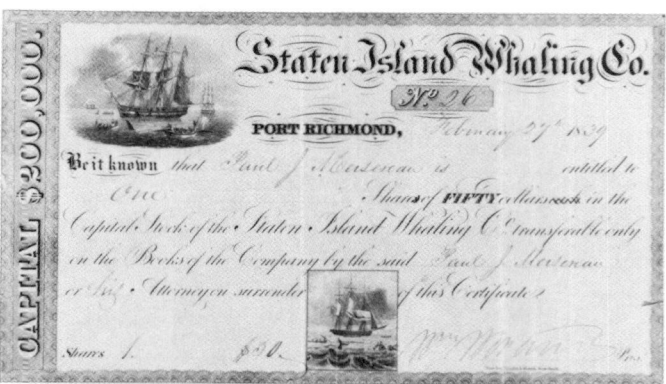

SHIPYARDS

From middle to late nineteenth century, the large amount of shipping passing Staten Island created an important shipbuilding and boatbuilding industry along the shores. At least one shipyard—that of Richard Lawrence—had operated on the island in the eighteenth century, but the scarcity of timber after the Revolution had led to a decline in the trade. The increase in maritime commerce and the growth of the oyster industry after the War of 1812, and the later development of recreational boating, brought about a revival of wooden craft construction and repair by midcentury.

Among the several prominent shipyards established on the island before 1850 was the one operated by William H. and James M. Rutan in Tottenville. In 1855 the Rutan yard employed twelve workers and was producing fifty schooners and forty-five sloops of various sizes.

There were seventeen shipbuilding firms on the island in 1880 (including three on the north shore, one in Stapleton, and eight in Tottenville). One hundred nineteen men were employed, constructing thirteen new vessels and twelve boats—mostly smacks, tugs, propeller yachts, and coal barges—and completing $87,400-worth of repair work in that year.

Constructing the four-masted schooner Tolima *at Carteret Shipyard, Travis, ca. 1910–12.*

Schooner *J. Simonson* of New York, Capt. Ellis, off Leghorn, Sept. 8, 1868, Lewis Renault, oil on canvas. *According to tradition, the transatlantic trade vessel depicted in this painting off the Italian coast in the Mediterranean was owned and operated by a Staten Island sea captain and shipping merchant and had been built on Staten Island at Rutan's Shipyard in Tottenville.*

THE RURAL ECONOMY

FACTORYVILLE

The New-York Dyeing and Printing Establishment. Illustration from advertising handbill (Lossing-Barritt, N.Y., engravers; Oliver & Brothers, 32 Beekman Street, New York City, printers) ca. 1856. An electrotype of the engraving with a brief description of the Factoryville dyeworks was published in the Staaten Islander *newspaper of February 16, 1856.*

The purchase in 1818 of a sixteen-acre parcel of farmland on the north shore by three New England industrialists and two Manhattan merchant-investors marked the beginning of a major change in the island's economy. The textile dye house and printing works founded in 1819 by brothers William and George M. Barrett and William Tileston of Boston and Samuel Whittemore and Farnham Hall of New York City on the site of what is now the intersection of Broadway and Richmond Terrace was one of the earliest and largest such operations in New York State. By 1824, when the business was incorporated as the New-York Dyeing and Printing Establishment, the company employed 100 to 150 workmen and had become the center of a growing community, the second new village—and the first large manufacturing center—to develop on the island in the nineteenth century.

Because of its uniqueness as a major industrial area and the predominance of the dyeworks as the center of the new community, the village was named Factoryville. The small body of fresh water that had long been known as Van Buskirk's Pond for the owner of the adjacent flour mill was redammed, enlarged, and rechristened Factory Pond.

In 1835 the dyeworks was the largest of the seven operating in the state, manufacturing $976,000-worth of finished products from $820,000 of raw materials annually and employing from 150 to 200 hands. The village of Factoryville had expanded along the Shore Road, Broadway, and the adjoining streets to include almost a hundred dwellings, and a second industrial plant, Charles Goodyear's manufactory for India rubber (gum elastic) cloth had also been founded.

Long after the community changed its name to West New Brighton in the early 1870s, its factories remained central features of the island landscape and major contributors to the island economy. Factoryville's growth provides the first example of a pattern later repeated elsewhere on Staten Island and throughout the New York metropolitan area.

THE DYEWORKS ARRIVE

Born in Concord, Massachusetts in 1775, William Barrett apprenticed to a clothier and established a textile dyeing business in Charlestown at the age of twenty-four. In 1804 he and his brother George M. Barrett opened a large dye house in Malden, Massachusetts, which, having little competition, soon became extremely profitable. Rebuilt after a disastrous fire in 1816, the Malden Dye House continued to operate and expand under the Barrett family name until the company dissolved in the early 1880s.

The early success of the Barrett Massachusetts enterprise appealed greatly to New York businessmen and political leaders during the period of intense nationalism that followed the War of 1812. When in September 1820 the Barrett, Tileston and Company Staten Island works were opened, the occasion was celebrated as an event of national significance. Among the officials who came to inspect the site and praise its operation as an important advance in domestic industry were the attorney general of the United States, the secretary of war, and the mayor of New York, one of whom raised a toast to "The Ladies and Gentlemen of New York and its vicinity—may they all resolve to dye on Staten Island."

At the time of founder William Barrett's death in 1834, the New-York Dyeing and Printing Establishment was still a unique enterprise. Over the next two decades under Samuel Marsh's direction, the dyeworks continued to prosper, but was forced to confront growing competition.

In 1820 the plant consisted of two structures, a 75' × 36' dyehouse, con-

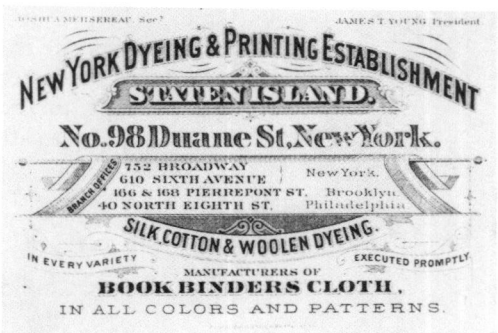

Memorial of . . . a Dyeing and Printing Establishment on Staten Island, January 19, 1824, printed by Gales and Seaton, 1824. SIIAS. This request by American merchants for government tariff advantages was read and referred to the Committee of Ways and Means of Congress. The petitioners, who had the support of the leading dealers in India goods in New York City, planned to dye and print cheap imported Indian fabrics and then sell the processed wares in the West Indies and South America. It is not known whether the request was granted.

Trade card of the New York Dyeing and Printing Establishment printed by F. L. M. Linder and Bauer, 10 Warren Street, New York City, ca. 1870.

New York & Staten Island Dye House, ink wash and pencil on paper ("drawn by G. Hayward for Doty engraver"), 1845. MCNY.

taining nineteen copper kettles and other machinery, and a 100' × 32' facility for finishing goods. "Broadcloths, cassimers, satins, lustrings, crapes, plush, silks, silk and cotton velvets, worsted cords, camels hair, silk and cotton shawls, hosiery, gloves, ladies and gentlemen's garments of every description" were dyed, and carpets, blankets, cotton and linen goods were cleaned to removed mildew and stains. An office in lower Manhattan, at 101 William Street, had been fitted up for receiving and delivering goods which were shipped directly to the Staten Island works.

By 1860 the company utilized eight steam engines, employed 160 male and 40 female workers and was processing 4,830,416 yards of cotton muslin, 55,268 pieces of silk, and $23,610-worth of consigned goods received from its three offices in Manhattan and one each in Brooklyn and Philadelphia.

THE SILK PRINTERS

Silk Printing, *reproduced from the American Magazine of Useful Knowledge (vol. 1, no. 10), 1829. N-YHS.*

The Irving Manufacturing Company, New Brighton, Photo Engraving Company, New York City, 1886.

To compensate for their lack of specialized knowledge in the field of textile printing, the officers of the New-York Dyeing and Printing Establishment imported skilled British craftsmen to work in their Staten Island factory. About 1830, John Crabtree, an English silk printer, emigrated to America to oversee the operations of the Factoryville plant silk printing department.

Crabtree succeeded in developing this branch of the industry, and in 1843 or 1844 he left the factory to found a silk printing plant of his own on Jersey Street in New Brighton. The new firm, known after 1848 as Crabtree and Wilkinson, specialized in the manufacture of colorfully printed silk handkerchiefs and bandannas, and quickly gained a considerable reputation in its field. By 1855 Crabtree and Wilkinson employed 183 workers (90 men, 3 women, 60 boys, and 30 girls) and was producing 1,520,000 handkerchiefs by both hand and steam power from 1,500 cases of raw silk annually. After Crabtree's death in 1863 the factory continued to operate into the 1870s under the direction of James Wilkinson and other members of the Crabtree family.

The plant was acquired in 1881 by the Irving Manufacturing Company, which adapted the site for the production of dress linings, India linens, Victoria lawns, tarlatanes, and mohair and silk plushes for upholstery.

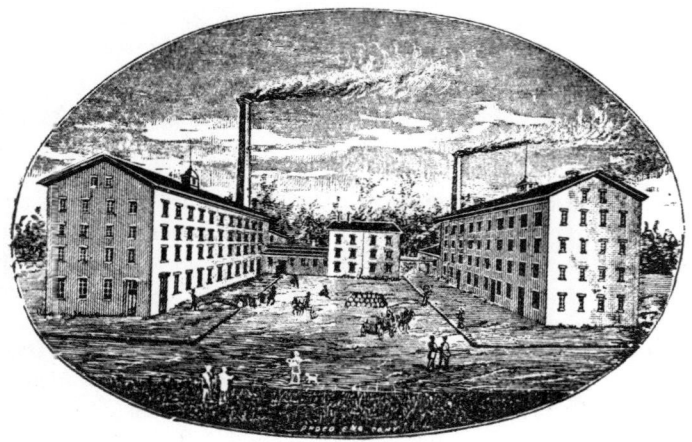

Block-printed silk bandana fragment attributed to the Crabtree and Wilkinson factory, New Brighton, ca. 1848–60.

THE COLONEL'S FACTORY

Col. Nathan Barrett (1795–1865), hand-tinted photograph, ca. 1860.

Barrett, Nephews dyeworks on Cherry Lane (Forest Avenue), showing dye yard and bleaching frames, photograph by F. L. Huff, Newark, ca. 1885.

In early 1850 a major dispute arose among the officers and managers of the New-York Dyeing and Printing Establishment on Staten Island. As a result, Col. Nathan Barrett, plant superintendent and a member of its founding family, withdrew from the company, purchased eight acres of land on Cherry Lane (now Forest Avenue), and started a rival firm in association with his three nephews—Nathan M., Joseph H., and Edwin B. Heal—and Abraham C. Wood.

Barrett, Nephews and Company's Staten Island Fancy Dyeing Establishment began operations in March 1851. The plant soon became known locally as "The Colonel's Factory," both to distinguish it from its predecessor, and in recognition of the prominent stature of the firm president, who was an active member of the local community.

Unlike the original Factoryville plant, which included silk and cotton printing in its operations, the works on Cherry Lane concentrated exclusively on dyeing, cleaning, and refinishing of silk, woolen, and fancy goods for the wholesale and retail markets. With its more modern, mechanized, steam-powered facility, the "fancy" dyeworks was extremely successful and soon threatened to overtake its rival.

After decades of successful competition with the new dyeworks, the once prosperous original factory began to fail by the 1880s. Both firms had greatly expanded their operations in the 1860s and 1870s, opening branch offices and agencies throughout the eastern United States, employing between four and six

Barrett, Nephews dyeworks on Cherry Lane (Forest Avenue), illustration from advertising handbill, 1882.

Advertising fly sheet, the Old Staten Island Dyeing Establishment, ca. 1895–1910.

Officers of the Barrett, Nephews dyeworks (Albert Heal, C. W. Kennedy, Baldwin Heal, Peter Heal), photograph by A. Struckman, ca. 1885.

hundred workers, adding vast amounts of costly machinery, and consuming hundreds of thousands of dollars worth of dyestuffs, water, and coal annually at each of their Staten Island plants.

In the early 1890s the older enterprise collapsed. The company was sold to a group of businessmen who immediately executed a merger with Barrett, Nephews and Company. The new, consolidated organization disposed of the Cherry Lane factory and, adopting the title Barrett, Nephews & Company, Old Staten Island Dyeing Establishment, Inc., returned in 1895 to its first location.

At the turn of the century some five hundred hands were employed by the consolidated firm, which in the years that followed became less of an industrial manufacturer and more of a large-scale textile cleaning service.

THE FACTORY VILLAGE

Capt. Henry Fountain (1783–1863), attributed to John Milburn (b. 1802, Great Britain, active in New York City, ca. 1850), oil on canvas, ca. 1820–40.

Fountain House Hotel, Richmond Terrace, West New Brighton, photograph by Charles Steinrock, ca. 1895.

The area around the first dyeworks developed rapidly into a thriving community center with a mixture of residential, industrial, and commercial features. What had started as a few coastal farmhouses, a ferry slip, a mill pond, and a small hotel had grown into a major village by 1850.

In the 1820s and 1830s the factory store operated by the dyeworks for its employees was probably the only commercial enterprise of its kind in the immediate vicinity. By the 1840s and 1850s, independent merchants and tradesmen were providing a wide variety of services in the area.

Near the establishment itself were erected rows of frame, and later brick, workers' houses, constructed and owned by the dyeworks and rented to employees. Close by were the substantial private homes of the factory managers and officers. Other manufacturers—of wallpaper, furniture, and carriages, for instance—also opened plants in the neighborhood, and one of the first volunteer fire departments on the island had been successfully organized.

Factoryville and environs, detail from map of Staten Island published by H. F. Walling, 1859.

Captain Henry Fountain (1783–1863) was a prominent Factoryville resident during the first half of the nineteenth century. He is best known as the owner and manager of the Fountain House, an eighteenth-century inn on the Shore Road that he acquired from the dyeworks in the late 1820s and operated as a hotel and meeting hall until the 1850s.

MIDCENTURY GROWTH

Arietta Street, Tompkinsville, C. Roche, oil on canvas, 1863. This lively scene depicts the village center of Tompkinsville looking west on Arietta Street from the ferry landing (up what is now Victory Boulevard from the shore below Bay Street). Among the once-prominent landmarks and business establishments included in the picture are: Wiener's Saloon (foreground right), Nautilus Hotel (left middle distance), steeple of the Reformed Protestant Dutch Church (center distance), and cupola of the Pavilion Hotel (on the hilltop). The figures in the foreground are said to be portraits of well-known Staten Islanders of the 1860s. Mr. and Mrs. Tompkins Westervelt appear on horseback and "Fatty" De Nyse, a local saloon keeper, is shown at the far left.

Adolph Schenck's Book and Job Printing Shop, 68 Broad Street, Stapleton, ca. 1890–95.

The changes of the 1810s and 1820s—the establishment of the first large-scale factories, the introduction of regular steam ferry service, and the development of suburban and industrial villages on the north and eastern shores—were a prelude for the more rapid transformation that occurred on the island in midcentury. By the beginning of the Civil War, major aspects of Staten Island's physical environment and the character and composition of its resident population had been fundamentally altered.

Between 1830 and 1860, the population increased by more than 250 percent—growing from a mere 7,082 to 25,492, and for the first time approaching the number of people stationed here during the Revolution. To the colonial village of Richmond and the early nineteenth-century developments at Tompkinsville and Factoryville had been added many other hamlets and towns throughout the north and east and along the south and west shores.

Between 1847 and 1851, more than a million immigrants, mostly from Ireland, the German states and other parts of northern Europe, landed at the port of New York. Several thousand of these new arrivals began to settle on Staten Island, especially in the rapidly expanding village centers, where they found work in the new factories or in new small businesses and commercial enterprises, providing needed services for other village residents.

Increased population brought along demands for increased housing, new occupations, and diversified services. To the traditional artisan workshops of the blacksmith, cordwainer, wheelwright, and cooper, and the mills, taverns, and inns of the preindustrial period were added groceries and drygoods stores, butcher and tailor shops, commercial bakeries, stationers, printers, tobacconists, tinsmiths, lumberyards, feed stores, and a wide variety of specialized trades and businesses, many catering to the particular needs or customs of recent immigrant groups. With the expansion of the north shore village centers, large hotels and resorts came banks, insurance agencies, law offices, and a call for better fire and police protection, and improved sanitation, health, and transportation services.

By 1860, when the long-awaited steam railway, running from Vanderbilt's Landing (Clifton) to Tottenville, had been completed, it was clear that Staten Island was developing in several different directions at once.

THE BREWERIES

Rubsam and Horrmann's Atlantic Brewery, Stapleton, photograph by George Bear, ca. 1895.

R & H Brewery parade wagon, photograph by George Bear, 1897.

One immediate result of the arrival of large numbers of German immigrants after the failure of the revolutions of 1848 was the establishment of an important new American industry—lager beer brewing. This distinctly German beverage, which is produced with a different kind of yeast than ale, stout, or porter, and requires a period of winter cooling before being marketed, was in great demand wherever the immigrants settled and soon became preferred by most other Americans as well.

Just after 1850 a series of lager breweries were established and began to flourish on Staten Island, in the areas of Clifton, Stapleton, and Castleton Corners. The island provided brewers with ready access to an expanding German-speaking population locally and in the immigrant communities of Manhattan and Brooklyn, with abundant sources of pure spring and well water, and with hillside caves for use as cool storage and fermentation vaults.

In 1851 the Clifton Brewery (later known as Bachmann's) was established—according to tradition by Antonio Meucci and Italian liberator Giuseppe Garibaldi. August Schmidt's Constanz Brewery (later Monroe Eckstein's) at Four Corners followed in 1852. The next year Bechtel's Brewery, the largest of the early establishments, opened in Stapleton. Bischoff's, a short-lived operation, followed in 1854, near Bechtel's; and in 1870 Joseph Rubsam and August

46 MADE ON STATEN ISLAND

Birthday certificate presented to August Horrmann (1835–1900) September 22, 1891. Leopold Steidel, artist, New York. This traditionally Germanic, commemorative certificate was presented to August Horrmann as a gift on his fifty-sixth birthday by friends and business associates at the Rubsam and Horrmann Brewery, Stapleton. Original watercolor vignettes illustrate important scenes in Horrmann's life: his birthplace (Frankfort-am-Main, Germany), the wholesale cheese store he owned and operated in Manhattan (1850–60), the Horrmann family's Manhattan townhouse (on the Bowery, 1865), the family's Stapleton, Staten Island residence (1891), the Atlantic (R & H) Brewery (built 1878), and the firm's first brewery (built 1870, destroyed by fire ca. 1878). The applied albumen photographs are portraits of August Horrmann and his partner, Joseph Rubsam (d. 1895).

Advertisement for the George Bechtel Brewing Co., Stapleton, on the reverse of Staten Island Electric Rail Road Co. ticket, 1892.

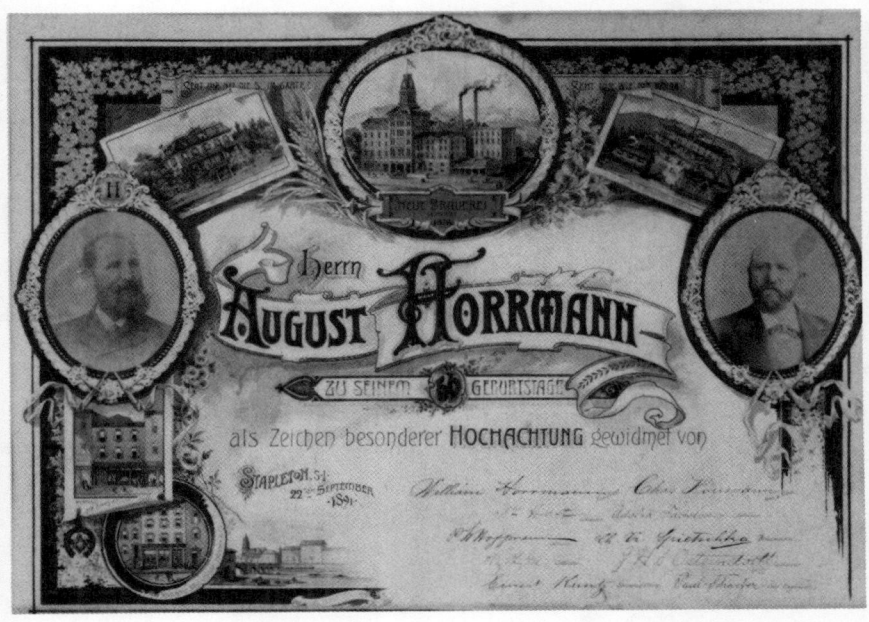

Horrmann established their Atlantic Brewery on Canal Street in Stapleton. Bechtel's, Bachmann's, and R & H were among the eleven firms awarded prizes at the Philadelphia Centennial Exposition; Bechtel's later gained an international reputation by winning awards in Paris and Sydney, Australia, and by being chosen by the Japanese ambassador for an order of 100,000 bottles to be sent to Japan.

By the late 1870s there were eight breweries in operation on the island, employing 363 adult male workers and producing more than 160,000 barrels of beer valued at $1,414,732 annually.

Illustration from trade card for Monroe Eckstein's Constanz Brewery, Four Corners, ca. 1880. MCNY.

Clifton Brewery, lithograph by N. Corradi printed by A. Weingartner, New York City, ca. 1851. Founded in 1851, Staten Island's first lager beer brewery, later known as Bachmann's, is believed to have been established by Italian immigrant Antonio Meucci with the assistance of exiled compatriot Giuseppe Garibaldi. The Clifton Brewery was located near the intersection of Lyndhurst Avenue and Ditson Street, Clifton.

BEER GARDENS AND RESORTS

The successful breweries were not just efficient manufacturing enterprises. To market and distribute their products the breweries acquired real estate holdings and developed close ties with the restaurant, recreation, and tourism businesses. The major breweries owned, operated, and rented saloons, taverns, beer gardens, hotels, and even resort complexes.

As early as 1860, the J. H. French gazetteer of New York State noted that Staten Island "has of late become a Sabbath day resort of the German population of New York City, thousands of whom repair every Sunday to the saloons and gardens attached to the breweries." By the end of the next decade the island was viewed by many New Yorkers as "a reservoir of Teutonic beer."

With the development of South Beach (in the 1880s) and Midland Beach (in the 1890s) as large-scale summer recreation areas, entertainment centers, and amusement parks the island brewing industry reached the peak of its fortune and influence.

Midland Beach, photograph by Ernest Seehuysen, ca. 1908.

Midland Beach Carousel, ca. 1914. Courtesy of Frederick Fried Archives. Begun on a small scale in the mid-1880s, Midland Beach was developed into an extensive resort complex by the Midland Terminal Company, a subsidiary of the organization that initiated electric trolley service to the area in 1896–7. The resort, which officially opened on August 29, 1896, grew rapidly, especially after the

(continued overleaf)

(continued from preceeding page) completion of a trolley line between Midland and South Beach in 1901.

Charles I. D. Looff (1852–1918) who built the Midland Beach Carousel, was a woodworking craftsman from Schleswig-Holstein, who emigrated to New York in 1870. Settling in Brooklyn, Looff worked as a woodcarver in a furniture factory and began producing carved, painted wooden animals during his spare time at home. When he assembled his figures into a merry-go-round on Coney Island in 1876, the result was an immediate success, which led him to open his own carousel factory in Brooklyn four years later. In addition to producing the Midland Beach Carousel, the Looff shop made at least one other in Coney Island; another for Young's Pier, Atlantic City; a ferris wheel at Rocky Point, Rhode Island; and huge carousels at Crescent Park and Goddard State Park, Rhode Island. Looff closed his Brooklyn factory in 1905–6, moving his family residence and business at first to Riverside, Rhode Island, and in 1910, to Ocean Park, California, where he continued to build numerous carousels, rides, piers, and casinos.

The Midland Beach Carousel managed to survive the many boardwalk fires that plagued the Staten Island beach resort and remained in operation until the 1940s or 1950s.

Poster for the Bachmann Brewing Company, Clifton, and Bachmann's South Beach, lithograph by Kihn and Hall, New York City, ca. 1890.

50 MADE ON STATEN ISLAND

Promotional photograph for Henry Carsten, bottler for Rubsam and Horrmann Brewing Company, Stapleton, photograph by George Bear, ca. 1890. As late as 1850, most breweries only sold directly to taverns or inns in hardwood kegs and barrels. Individuals who wanted to drink beer at home or elsewhere had to bring their pots or buckets to a saloon. The first bottles for beer, produced and marketed in the 1850s and 1860s, closely resembled soda and mineral water containers. By 1870, however, a distinctive beer bottle shape—a tall, long neck "blob-top" form—had been established and was in widespread use. These mold-blown bottles often bear the embossed name of a brewery, an independent bottler, or a hotel or tavern.

"Calendar Girl" poster for Rubsam and Horrmann Brewing Company, Stapleton, 1891.

SODA, SELTZER, AND BOTTLING WORKS

At the same time that breweries and beer bottlers were expanding their operations throughout the United States, a related (and ultimately rival) industry was also emerging. The marketing of non-alcoholic, effervescent (bubbly) bottled beverages began on a very small scale in the late-18th century, when Americans discovered the supposedly medicinal properties of the natural mineral spring waters of Saratoga and other areas. Around 1830, artificially carbonated or "soda" water became popular; the addition of various flavorings and the invention of the "soda fountain" during the decade that followed secured the success of this development. By 1859 there were at least three soda water manufacturers and bottlers in business on Staten Island—James Larkin (Port Richmond), James Coles (Castleton), and Charles Warnecke (Castleton).

The Hadkins Bottling Company was founded in Perth Amboy, New Jersey in 1863 by John H. Hadkins and Charles Low. Shortly afterwards, Hadkins purchased Low's interest in the firm and in 1867 moved the plant across the Arthur Kill to Tottenville, Staten Island. By the late nineteenth century, Hadkins was the largest bottling company on Staten Island and one of the foremost businesses of its kind in greater New York. The works continued under family ownership until operation ceased in the late 1940s.

Advertising card for the Hadkins Bottling Company, Tottenville, ca. 1887.

Letterhead of Charles Walter & Son, importers of "First Quality Bohemian Siphons and manufacturers of Walter's Patented Siphon Heads," Stapleton, ca. 1900–10.

CABINETMAKING

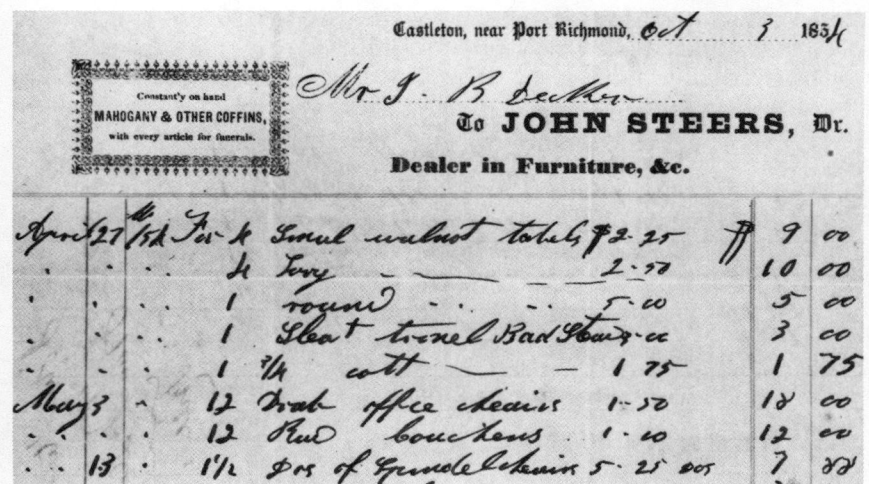

Bill of sale of John Steers, Castelton dealer in furniture and coffins, to J. B. Decker, October 3, 1854.

Sewing table, attributed to the shop of John Steers, West New Brighton, ca. 1850. This sewing table was used by the Jones, Prall, or Decker family, Northfield.

Furniture-making as a specialized trade and small-scale Staten Island industry was a product of ninteenth-century village growth. Prior to the 1820s, most islanders' common household furniture needs could be provided by woodworking farmer-artisans and rural carpenters; finer, high-style pieces were purchased in Manhattan, Philadelphia, or from New Jersey village shops. Beginning in the 1830s and 1840s "manufactories" of simple, inexpensive domestic and commercial furniture were established in the north and eastern shore population centers.

John Steers (1830–1898) was brought to Staten Island from England by his parents in 1842. After a short apprenticeship with a Newark cabinetmaker, he opened his own business in Factoryville as a furniture-maker and undertaker. There were three men working in John Steers' shop in 1860, producing mahogany bureaus and coffins valued at $5,000. In later years his business turned more exclusively to retail sales, and then undertaking, while his cousin, Thomas Steers (1833–1923), and nephew Charles Steers (b. 1863) continued the family tradition of cabinetmaking into the 1940s.

CARRIAGE MANUFACTURING

John F. Schwiebert's (earlier I. M. Marsh's and Marsh & Nolan's) Richmond Wagon Works, Richmond Road; photograph by Empire Photo View Company, ca. 1900–10.

Buggy from advertisement for P. J. Brown Carriage Company, West New Brighton, engraving by Wood and Roberts, 1886.

The manufacture of horse-drawn carriages, wagons, and carts required a large, specialized workplace and the combined knowledge and skills of a variety of wood- and metal-working trades. While one fine coachmaker, James Weir, is known to have owned property on the island before 1800, and rural wheelwrights' and blacksmiths' shops repaired and fabricated vehicles during the early nineteenth century, carriagemaking did not become an important business until just before 1850.

Staten Island's first large carriage factory was established in the late 1840s in the village of Richmond by Isaac Marsh, who had moved from Essex County, New Jersey earlier in the decade. By 1855 Marsh's shop was employing five boys and fourteen adult men and producing about sixty carriages yearly. A number of other island carriage makers started as apprentices in Marsh's works, which continued operating under various owners until, after several years of use as an auto body shop, its business ceased in 1939.

In 1880 there were six principal carriage and wagon works, employing fifty-one men, on the island. As the century progressed, these concerns became more strictly assemblers and repairers of mass-produced vehicle parts than actual manufacturers of carriages.

P. J. Brown Carriage Company office and repository in the former West Brighton Public School building, Elizabeth and Cary Avenues, ca. 1900. After working in the New Haven carriage-building firm of Lawrence, Bradley and Company and spending six years with J. B. Brewster and Company in New York, Philip J. Brown (1838–1911) returned to his native Rahway, New Jersey in 1866 and started a manufactory of his own. When his shop was destroyed by fire in 1872, he moved to Staten Island. Two years later he reopened his business on Richmond Terrace, West New Brighton.

The P. J. Brown Carriage Company carried on an active trade in the manufacture, sale, and rental of carriages and "business and contractors' dumping wagons and carts" becoming the largest Staten Island enterprise of its kind by 1896, with a reputation that extended to New York, Bayonne, and Brooklyn. In the 1880s the firm expanded its livery business, which was ultimately incorporated separately as the Richmond Storage Warehouse and Van Company. After 1900 the carriage works branched out into automobile sales, fitting, and repairs. Although the carriage company was dissolved in 1914, the storage and warehouse business continues in operation today.

Harold Applegate in his donkey cart made by Michael Duff, Port Richmond, ca. 1898. In addition to the major carriage-making establishments—Marsh & Nolan, P. J. Brown, R. Lemmer & Co., Wille & Hein, Henry Schwenck, and Oscar Dahlberg—which employed between a dozen and twenty-five workers, a number of much smaller, independent shops existed on the island. Duff, who may have also worked in one of the larger shops, listed himself as a carriage-and wagonmaker with a shop on Post Avenue, near Jewett, Port Richmond, in the 1898 Staten Island business directory.

This small child's donkey cart, made and signed by Duff, is one of a miniscule number of fully documented island-made vehicles known to survive. The cart was owned by, and probably made for, young Harold Applegate of Port Richmond, who carved his initials into it on March 6, 1903.

Interior view of C. A. Scheiper's Wagon Works, Bay Street, Tompkinsville, 1918. Courtesy of Herman Scheiper.

LOUIS ETTLINGER & SONS

Louis Ettlinger & Sons factory, Richmond Avenue, Graniteville, ca. 1900. From the 1952 Staten Island Chamber of Commerce Yearbook.

Painted tin Ettlinger factory sign, ca. 1900–10.

In 1854, about four years after arriving in New York from Gernsbach, Germany, Louis Ettlinger brought his family to Graniteville, Staten Island, where he began to manufacture boxes for use in the retail jewelry trade. Starting as a small cottage industry, the family-run firm pioneered the development of the satin and velvet-lined paper box and grew to become one of the foremost manufacturers of jewelry boxes in the country. The Ettlinger factory on Richmond Avenue eventually produced most of the velvet, silk, satin, leather, and paper boxes for Manhattan's leading jewelers, silversmiths, stationers, perfumers, caterers, and department stores. During its peak years of operation, around 1900, the firm employed only about one hundred men and women, some of whom worked at home. Louis Ettlinger & Sons remained in operation on Staten Island for 104 years, finally going out of business in 1958.

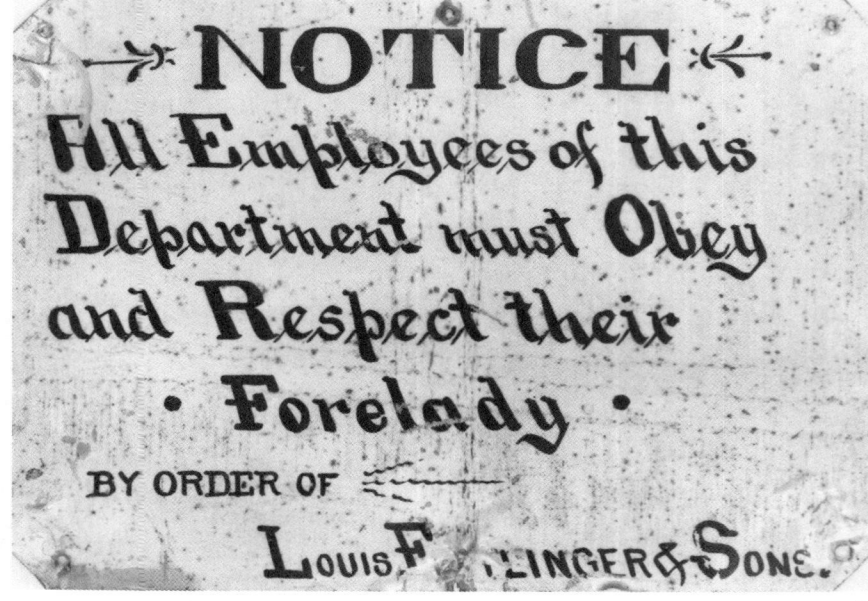

LOUIS DEJONGE & COMPANY

Four or five years after establishing themselves in Manhattan as importers and manufacturers of specially coated, or "fancy," papers, the brothers Julius and Louis Dejonge opened a large factory on Staten Island. The J. & L. Dejonge Fancy Paper Staining and Marble Paper Steam Works began operation on Richmond Turnpike (now Victory Boulevard) in Tompkinsville about 1850 and immediately became one of the island's leading industries.

The Dejonge plant was one of the earliest in America to utilize European methods for the production of fine gift, art, and commercial papers by means of surface tinting and glazing; it was the first factory in the country to make white coated lithograph paper.

In 1855 the Dejonge factory was producing 10,400 reams of stained and coated papers, valued at $260,000 annually, and employing sixty workers (twenty adult men, twenty adult women, ten boys, and ten girls). Five years later, the workforce had expanded to ninety (forty men and fifty women). By the mid-1880s, the firm, known as Louis Dejonge & Company, employed 250 hands, produced "every description of stained and fancy papers used for lithographic printing, book linings, trunk linings, box covering, etc." at a rate of six tons a day, or 100,000 reams annually, and was also marketing fine bookbinders' supplies, leather, and cloth. By the 1890s the plant, with four hundred workers, was considered one of the largest such manufacturers in the country.

In 1918 the Dejonge factory moved from Tompkinsville to a new and enlarged fireproof building at the corner of Tompkins and Simonson Avenues, Clifton, where it remained in operation until the mid-1970s.

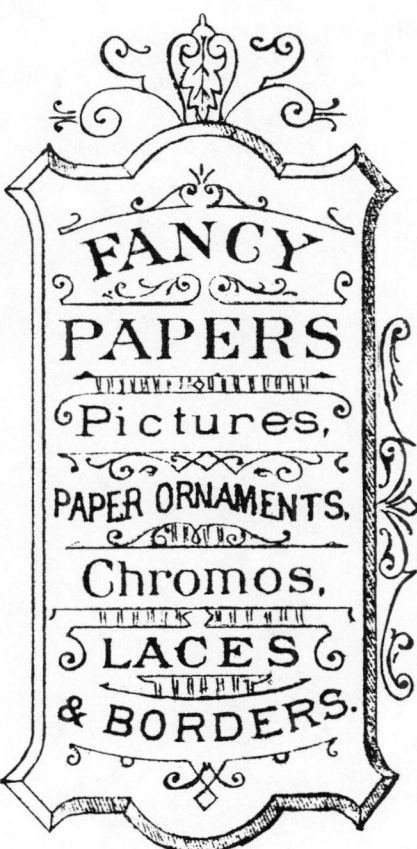

Louis Dejonge & Company factory on Staten Island from Dejonge billhead, 1901.

Cover detail from Dejonge fancy paper sample book with silver- and gold-coated and textured papers, ca. 1870–80.

CLAY MINES AND BRICK WORKS

New York Anderson Pressed Brick Company stock certificate, Goer & Quensel, Lithographers, Chicago, 1890. SIIAS.

Cover of B. Kreischer & Company price list, ca. 1860–76. SIIAS.

The existence of valuable clay and kaolin deposits on the southwest shore and along the Fresh Kill from its mouth to Greenridge, and rich, but smaller, claybeds in the Elm Park section of the north shore led to the development of a major brick manufacturing industry before 1860. The earliest, largest, and most influential of these establishments was the one founded in 1854 by Balthazar Kreischer along the Arthur Kill just south of Rossville.

Kreischer (1813–1886) had emigrated to Manhattan from Germany just after the great New York fire of 1835. With a background in the construction trades, he assisted in the rebuilding of the city, and in 1845 was involved in the establishment of a factory for the production of firebrick in lower Manhattan. His search for a reliable supply of local clay brought him to the Staten Island west shore, where he purchased land, started mines, and opened a second fac-

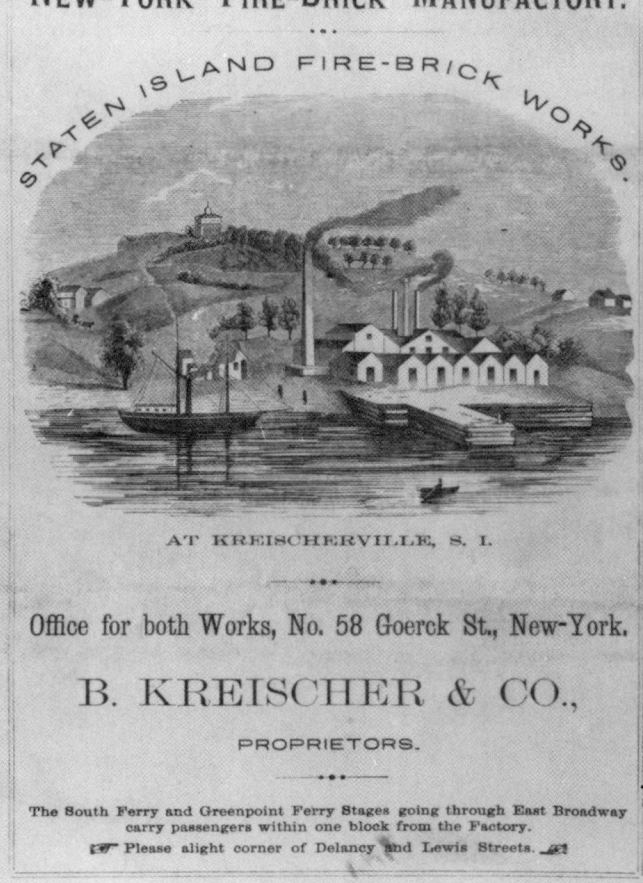

Barnard College (Columbia University) near Broadway and 116 Street in New York City, built with Kreischer decorative terra cotta, ca. 1900. MCNY.

Employees at the New York Anderson Pressed Brick Company, Kreischerville, ca. 1890.

tory in 1855. In 1860 the island plant employed sixty men and was producing a million firebricks valued at $300,000 annually. Around the works arose a village, called (until World War I) Kreischerville, where the founder built an estate house and matching mansions for his sons, who became partners in the firm.

In 1876 the island plant was expanded and the Manhattan works closed. Experiments were attempted in porcelain manufacture (in the early 1880s) and architectural terra cotta (the late 1890s), but the industry's strength remained the production of firebrick, clay retorts and blocks, and the ornamental molded brick produced by the Kreischer-owned Anderson Pressed Brick works after 1886. At the height of its operations in the late 1890s, B. Kreischer & Sons employed more than three hundred workers and turned out 3,500,000 bricks yearly. Kreischer brick, which continued to be produced until the 1930s, was used on major building projects throughout the New York metropolitan area.

Double pug mill with belt for feeding clay at B. Kreischer & Sons, Kreischerville; photograph by Henry Ries reproduced in Clays of New York: Bulletin of the New York State Museum *(Albany, 1900).*

PRINT-CUTTING AND WALLPAPER MANUFACTURE

The New York area rapid midcentury growth created a large market for inexpensive, industrially produced domestic ornament and interior decoration. Between the 1840s and 1860s, two new industries, wallpaper manufacturing and print- or block-cutting, developed on the Staten Island north shore.

In 1849 Thomas B. Smith established a wallpaper works in the Factoryville plant previously occupied by Charles Goodyear's failed New York India Rubber Cloth Company. The firm, known in the 1860s as T. B. & R. Smith, employed about forty men and ten women and produced 1,800,000 pieces of machine-printed wallpapers and 120,000 yards of oil floorcloth a year at the height of its operations. From the 1870s until it closed around the turn of the century the factory was run under the direction of Mrs. M. A. Baldwin Douglas—making it one of the only nineteenth century island industries to be owned and managed by a woman. In the mid-1890s the Baldwin Douglas factory employed forty hands and produced two million rolls of wallpaper annually.

Print- or block-cutting—the manufacture of blocks and rollers for printing wallpaper, textiles, and floor coverings—is a highly skilled handcraft that developed in close association with these other industries. In 1869, John Westbrook founded a block-cutting firm next to the Smiths' wallpaper plant in Factoryville. Westbrook's shop, which was continued by his sons into the early twentieth century, was later bought out by Johnston L. Rose, who created in 1912 the Macrae and Rose Print Cutting Company. The Macrae and Rose factory, on Broadway, West New Brighton, was at one time the nation's largest block-cutting establishment, employing sixty men during the rush season. The entire, enormously time-consuming process— initial sketching, tracing and transferring of design to the rollers or blocks (one for each color), cutting and fitting of the minute brass strips (shaped to conform to the design) for each roller, and filling of the brass outlinets with prepared felt—took place under one roof. This unique industry finally terminated in 1958.

Opposite: Design for wallpaper by Clinton F. Allen, designer, block-cutter, and sketchman at Macrae and Rose Print Cutting Company, West New Brighton, watercolor on paper, ca. 1940. Clinton F. Allen (1905–) carried on the skills of the block-cutting trade until the industry terminated in the late 1950s. Born on Staten Island, Allen was employed at Macrae and Rose from 1919 to 1950, working as block-cutter, sketchman, and designer. The design pattern, drawn with oily black ink on transparent paper, was burnished onto rollers. Craftsmen would chisel beside the pattern lines and then gradually hammer into place shaped brass that duplicated the original design and formed the printing surface.

T. B. & R. Smith's wallpaper and oil cloth printing factory, State and High Streets, Factoryville (West New Brighton), ca. 1870.

MIDCENTURY GROWTH

INDUSTRIAL STATEN ISLAND

Arthur Kill Bridge from S. C. Judson Illustrated Sketch Book of Staten Island..., 1886.

The Standard Varnish works, Elm Park, ca. 1911.

Immediately following the Civil War, heavy industries continued to develop on the island, expanding with increasing rapidity after the 1880s. Advocates of further industrialization promoted Staten Island as a "field for new industries" "because of her Excellent Location, Remarkable Resources, and Superior Natural Advantages." The latter, as enumerated by the Staten Island Chamber of Commerce from 1896 to 1898, were:

FIRST—Progressive public spirit, encouraging in every way the establishment of new industries.

SECOND—The extraordinary advantages of being located on and forming a part of New York Harbor.

THIRD—Exceptionally good facilities for the receipt of raw material by rail or water from all points of the United States and from foreign countries.

FOURTH—Excellent shipping facilities by canal, ocean, and rail to all parts of the United States and to Europe.

FIFTH—Low price of manufacturing sites accessible by rail or water, or by both.

SIXTH—The close proximity of New York City, with its enormous purchasing power of manufactured goods for home consumption, for distribution and for export.

SEVENTH—Cheap fuel.

EIGHTH—An abundant supply of all classes of labor (available on Staten Island, in New York, Brooklyn, and New Jersey).

NINTH—The moderate cost of living and low rents for employees, combined with all the advantages of an old-established, well-regulated community.

In 1880 there were 100 principal manufacturing establishments on Staten Island employing 1,557 persons (1,439 males over 16; 88 females over 15; and 30 children or youths) and producing $4,635,237-worth of finished goods from $2,807,237-worth of materials annually. By the 1920s, the number of industrial plants had almost tripled, the factory workforce numbered over 15,000, and there were at least two companies employing more than 1,000 people.

C. W. HUNT COMPANY

The overwhelming international significance of coal as an energy source in the late nineteenth century contributed to the rise of a major island industry. Settling on Staten Island after the Civil War, Charles Wallace Hunt (1841–1911) established a retail coal business near the old dyeworks in West Brighton and began to develop improved mechanical means for unloading, transporting, and storing heavy, bulk materials. The success of his early designs led Hunt to begin manufacturing and marketing his inventions and improvements.

Founded in 1872 and incorporated fourteen years later, the C. W. Hunt Company became one of the island's largest and most famous industrial establishments by the turn of the century. Hunt was issued 147 patents during his lifetime, and the products from his West Brighton factory were used in every major port, mining region, and U.S. naval station around the world. His plant manufactured coal-handling machinery; automatic and cable industrial railways and conveyor systems; steam shovels and boilers; hoisting engines and

Opposite left: C. W. Hunt Company promotional photograph of machine shop foreman A. S. Granger in coal dump bucket, ca. 1900–10.

Opposite right: C. W. Hunt Company office staff, West New Brighton, 1910.

C. W. Hunt Company assembling room interior, West New Brighton, ca. 1900–10.

blocks; industrial grade manila hoisting and transmission rope; storage battery trucks; electric locomotives; and a wide range of related items.

With the expiration of Hunt's patents and the founder's death shortly thereafter, the company lost its competitive edge and began a decline that was completed by the Great Depression.

EVERY BRANCH OF INDUSTRY

"We have 175 industrial plants [on Staten Island], employing 35,000 persons, covering every branch of manufacture, among which are some of the largest concerns in the country," boasted the Port Richmond Board of Trade in 1922. Fireworks; chemicals, colors, and dyes; paints, oils and varnishes; metals and metal products; building materials; packaged foods, beverages, and patent medicines were just some of the products of island factories, foundries, quarries, and processing plants between the 1870s and the 1930s.

In 1876 J. B. King established the "Windsor Plaster Mills" on the New Brighton shorefront to receive and process the raw gypsum rock shipped from the company quarries in Windsor, Nova Scotia. Next door to and in association with the plaster mills, the Muralo Company, producers of water-base paint and sanitary wall finishes, opened a factory in 1894. J. B. King & Co. was acquired

Advertisement for the Muralo Company, New Brighton, from Richmond Borough: Its Real Estate, Railroads, Trolleys, Improvements and Industries . . . , *1906.*

Detail of J. B. King's Windsor Plaster Mills letterhead, ca. 1895.

70 MADE ON STATEN ISLAND

Standard Varnish parade float for the Hudson-Fulton Celebration on Staten Island, photograph by Charles Steinrock, 1909.

Unexcelled Fireworks sales catalogue printed by D. A. Hailman, St. Louis, 1889.

by U.S. Gypsum in 1924 and the works, always a sizeable operation, were expanded into the largest mills of their kind in the country. Nearby, the white lead works, which was founded in 1842 as John Jewett and Sons and acquired before 1900 by the National Lead Company, continued to operate under the Dutch Boy trademark.

In the 1890s and the first decade of the 1900s, many other large manufacturing concerns opened plants on Staten Island. The Standard Varnish works relocated its Long Island factory in Mariner's Harbor in 1892. Benjamin Lowenstein moved his small scrap metal concern to the island in 1900 and created the Tottenville Copper Company. In 1907–8 the German pigment manufacturers, G. Siegle Corporation, constructed a factory for their American operations in Rosebank. This unique plant, which developed and produced high-quality synthetic colors for ink, cosmetics, paints, and dyes, was taken over by the U.S. government during World War I and merged in the 1920s with the Ansbacher Corporation of Brooklyn.

PORT IVORY

Port Ivory pumphouse under construction, ca. 1907. Courtesy of The Procter & Gamble Company Archives, Cincinnati.

Founded in Cincinnati in 1837 the commercial soapmaking firm of Procter & Gamble first achieved national prominence in 1879 with the development and highly successful marketing of Ivory soap. Just after 1900 the company embarked on an intensive expansion program to extend its manufacturing operations beyond its Ohio home and headquarters. A second factory was opened in Kansas City in 1904, and a year later, after careful study of the New York area, a 77-acre parcel on the Kill Van Kull at Howland Hook, Staten Island was chosen as the site for a new eastern plant.

Port Ivory, named in honor of the company's premier product, began operation in October 1907, producing Ivory and Lenox bar soaps at a rate of one million cases per year. The initial eleven buildings of the factory complex were constructed by the Milliken Brothers Structural Iron Works and Rolling Mill of Howland Hook. A workforce of four hundred employees, led by a supervisory crew that had been personally selected from the Ivorydale (Cincinnati) and Kansas City plants by company president William Cooper Procter, started up the works, which grew rapidly.

In 1912 a large building for the new soap powder production was added, followed shortly by new warehouse and power facilities. When construction of the Crisco Building began in 1926, the plant already employed 1,100 and had been enlarged to twenty-eight buildings on a 129-acre site. By the late 1920s, Port Ivory—with a workforce of 1,500; a production line that not only included framed bar soaps, packaged soap chips, flakes, granules, and powder but food shortening and subsidiary processing of "oil meal" for fertilizer and animal feed and kegs, tubs, barrels, crates and boxes for storage and shipping; extensive docks; four miles of railroad tracks and two switching locomotives—was one of the largest industrial plants and employers on Staten Island.

The Procter & Gamble plant at Port Ivory, photograph by Fairchild Aerial Surveys, Inc., 1927.

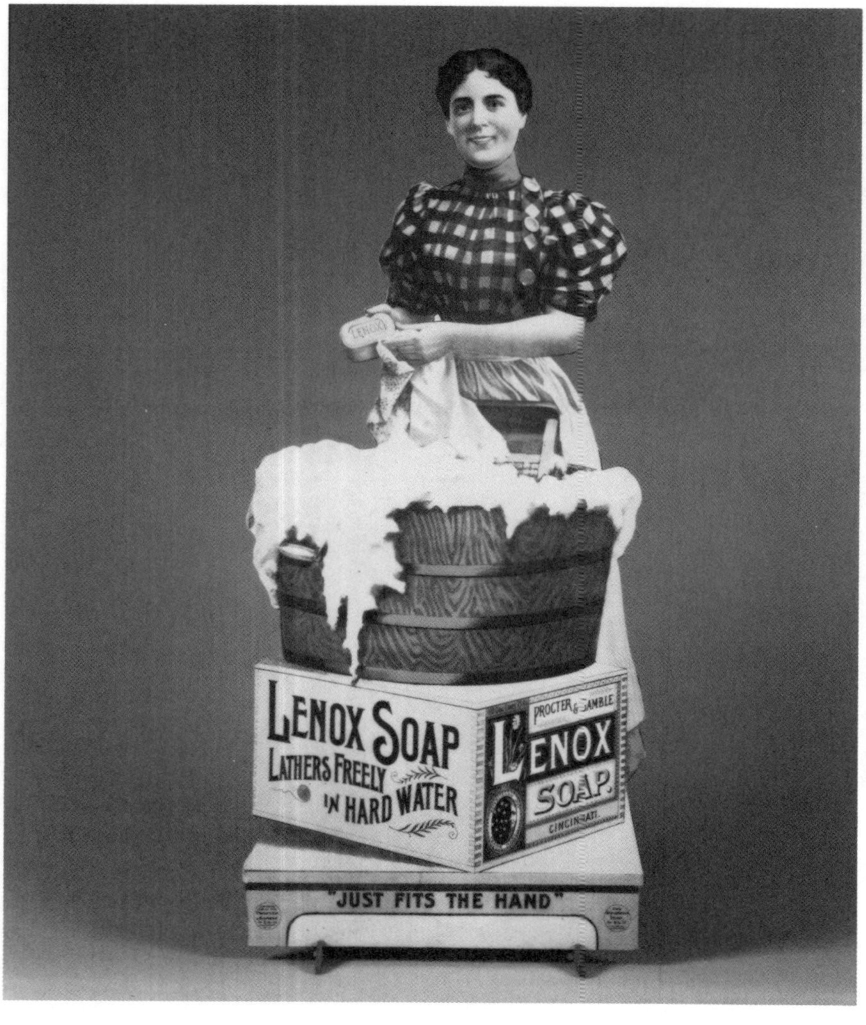
LENOX
LENOX SOAP
LATHERS FREELY IN HARD WATER
PROCTER & GAMBLE
LENOX
SOAP
CINCINNATI
"JUST FITS THE HAND"

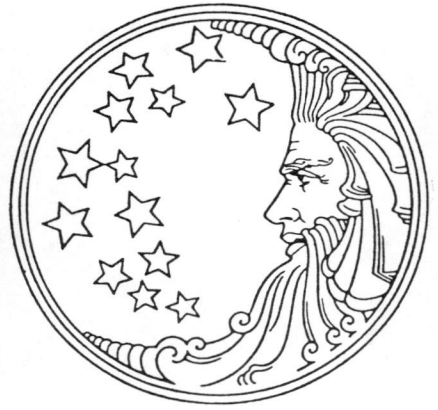

"Lenox Girl" advertising display of Procter & Gamble Company, Strobridge Litho Company, Cincinnati and New York, 1898. Courtesy of The Procter & Gamble Company Archives, Cincinnati.

Procter & Gamble trademark depicting the man in the moon: first registered 1882, final design 1932. Courtesy of The Procter & Gamble Company Archives, Cincinnati.

Star Naphtha packing line at Port Ivory, 1919. Courtesy of The Procter & Gamble Company Archives, Cincinnati.

INDUSTRIAL STATEN ISLAND

THE FACTORY BY THE SEA

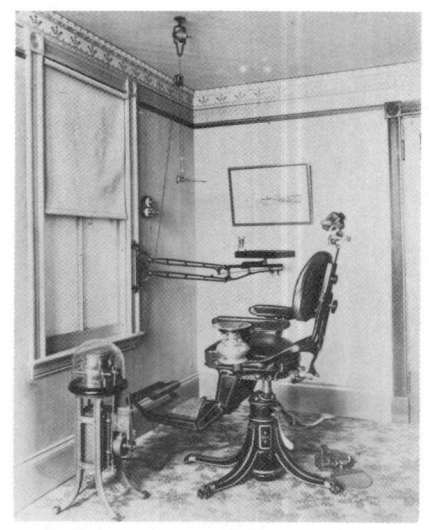

S. S. White dentist's chair and motor stand with ceiling suspension, ca. 1910. Courtesy of Joseph Helmer.

Prince's Bay Beach, photograph by W. J. Grimshaw, ca. 1920.

About 1865 Algernon K. Johnston purchased the buildings and docks at Seguine's Point (Prince Bay) that had served for more than a decade as a palm oil processing and candle works. Here, with his brothers Melville M. and William A., he established a small specialized factory for the manufacture of dental supplies and equipment.

In 1881 a new corporation, the S. S. White Dental Manufacturing Company, was created, when Johnston Brothers merged with the large Philadelphia-based firm that had been founded thirty-seven years earlier by Dr. Samuel Stockton White (1822–1879). With this consolidation, the patent interests of the two concerns were harmonized and the entire organization and operating force of the Prince Bay factory was retained under the direction of its former owners. Major additions to the plant in 1888–9, 1901, and 1903 enabled an enormous increase in the size and scope of production. By the late 1890s, S. S. White was not only the foremost manufacturing enterprise on the south shore, but actually the largest-employing, most diversified industry on the entire island. Amalgams; gold foil and fillings; bottled anesthetic gas; rubber denture bases; dental chairs, drills, cuspidors, and burs; and much of the machinery used in the manufacturing processes themselves were just some of the items produced in the plant. There were 425 men and women working in

S. S. White bur department, Prince Bay, ca. 1922. Courtesy of Joseph Helmer.

Female employees dancing in the S. S. White employee lounge, Prince Bay, ca. 1920. Courtesy of Joseph Helmer.

S. S. White softball team at Rhinehart Oval, Pleasant Plains, 1951. Courtesy of Joseph Helmer.

Workers at the S. S. White Dental Manufacturing Company, Prince Bay, ca. 1880. Courtesy of Joseph Helmer.

the factory in 1896; between 600 and 700 in 1906; and 1,800 to 1,900 in 1927. Employee comfort, safety, and the healthfulness of the work environment were prime concerns of the organization, which prided itself with its familial atmosphere; recreational, food, and dental clinic facilities; and the lengthy terms of service of large numbers of its employees. For more than a century, "The Factory by the Sea" remained a unique enterprise in an area better known for its beaches, farms, and oyster beds, than huge, complicated industries.

ATLANTIC TERRA COTTA

Modeling crew at Atlantic Terra Cotta Company plant No. 1, Tottenville, ca. 1900–24.

In the aftermath of the disastrous urban fires in Chicago (1871) and Boston (1872), American builders, engineers, and architects found in terra cotta a fire-resistant, lightweight cladding and construction material that was extremely versatile and relatively inexpensive. Terra cotta, literally "cooked, or burnt earth," is a high-heat-fired, porous natural clay (or earthenware) that can be produced in a wide variety of ornamental forms, shapes, hues, and textures.

For over three decades the Atlantic Terra Cotta Works, Tottenville, designed and manufactured architectural fabric and ornament, sculpture, and garden pottery that was installed and used in almost every major American city and even in Japan. Founded in 1897 by former craftsmen and officers of the highly successful Perth Amboy Terra Cotta Company just across the Arthur Kill, Atlantic opened its factory on East Broadway, Tottenville, in 1898 and expanded rapidly. By 1906 the Tottenville plant, which had grown from its initial three to eight kilns, was employing 450 to 500 men and was producing the fabric and ornament for such prestigious projects as the first New York City subway stations, the upper stories of the Flatiron Building, and the Plaza Hotel.

In 1907 the Tottenville works combined with the huge Perth Amboy plant and the smaller Excelsior Company of Rocky Hill, New Jersey to form the expanded, incorporated Atlantic Terra Cotta Company. Under the new consolidated organization the Tottenville plant was known as No. 1; Perth Amboy became No. 2; Rocky Hill was No. 3; and the Standard Terra Cotta Works in Perth Amboy, acquired shortly afterwards, became No. 4. The Atlanta Terra Cotta Company in East Point, Georgia, also owned by the corporation, was administered separately. During the industry's heyday before the Great Depression, Atlantic was the largest enterprise of its kind in the world.

Woolworth Building, Broadway and Park Place, New York City, ca. 1925. MCNY.

Advertisement for the Atlantic Terra Cotta Works, Tottenville, 1906.

INDUSTRIAL STATEN ISLAND

TERRA COTTA DESIGN AND PRODUCTION

Atlantic designed and produced both stock terra cotta pieces and materials made to special order. Based on architects' proposals, plans, and specifications, company designers developed sketches and draftsmen prepared detailed shop drawings, allowing for the shrinkage of the materials during firing (approximately one inch per foot). Skilled model-makers sculpted the designs in clay, which were then cast in plaster to produce molds for the manufacturing process. A mixture of New Jersey clays (more suitable for terra cotta than the Staten Island varieties) and a "grog" of ground, fired ceramic materials was hand-pressed and smoothed into the molds in uniform layers and allowed to dry. Once removed from the molds, the clay pieces were dried further, glazed or sprayed with pigment if a surface coating was desired, and fired in huge kilns in which the temperature was precisely controlled. After cooling, the pieces were checked and marked to insure proper joining and then packed for shipment.

The laborers and skilled craftsmen at the Tottenville works, many of whom were recent immigrants from Germany, Italy, and eastern Europe, often traveled to the other company plants to work on contract or assist with particular orders.

Opposite: Model makers, Atlantic Terra Cotta Company, Tottenville, photograph by Herman Guether, 1924. Courtesy of William Guether.

Drafting room, Atlantic Terra Cotta Company plant No. 1, Tottenville, 1924. Courtesy of Vera M. Sieger. The drafting department chief, Karl A. Sieger (ca. 1886–1979), is standing right of center (wearing suspenders).

Spray room, Atlantic Terra Cotta Company plant No. 1, Tottenville, probably photographed by Herman Guether, ca. 1910–25. Courtesy of William Guether.

Rudolf Weisman in modeling room of Atlantic Terra Cotta Company, Tottenville, ca. 1915–25. Courtesy of Audrey Hacker.

Atlantic Terra Cotta construction and jointing details, 1925.

Stock design from Atlantic Terra Cotta promotional order catalogue, ca. 1925. Courtesy of Vera M. Sieger.

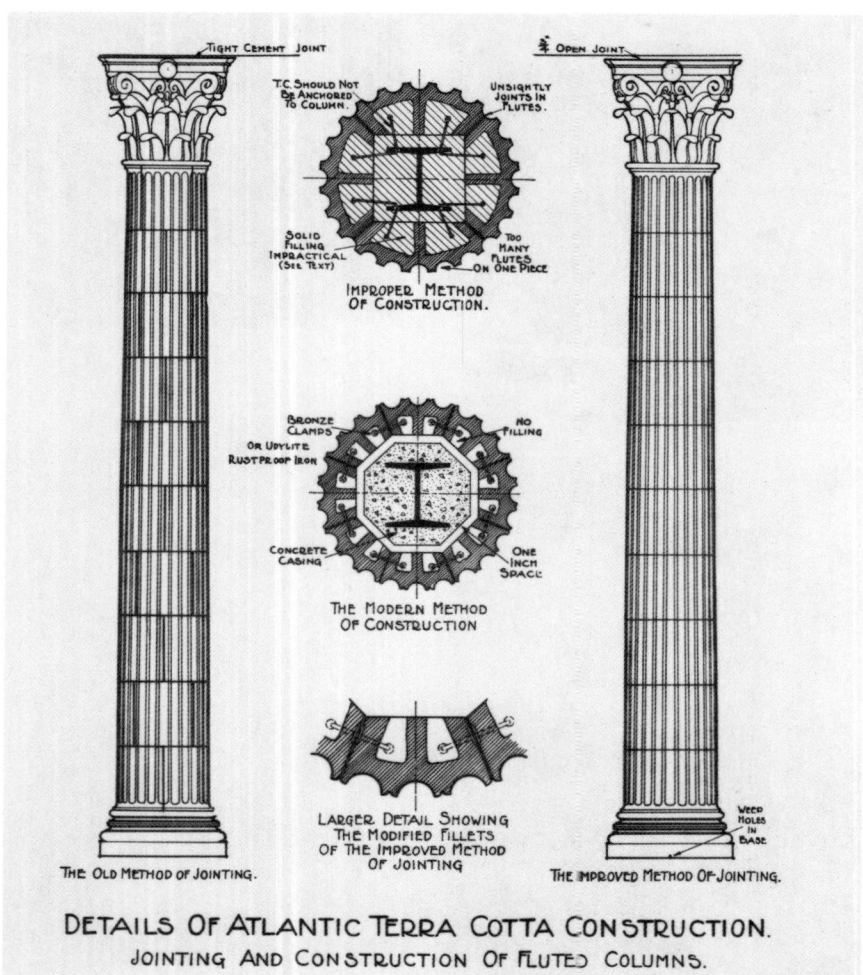

Installation of Atlantic Terra Cotta roofing tiles and crest ornaments at the Philadelphia Museum of Art, ca. 1926–8. Courtesy of Rocky Hill Community Group, Rocky Hill, New Jersey.

MAYER'S CONFECTIONERY

Vienna Biscuit box label, Gustav A. Mayer, manufacturer, Stapleton, ca. 1870–90.

The various specialized manufacturing enterprises undertaken by Gustav A. Mayer around the turn of the twentieth century are representative of a whole field of small local industries that were once common throughout the New York area.

Born near Ulm, Germany in 1845, Mayer apprenticed in the confectionery trade and, after traveling in Germany and Switzerland, emigrated to New York City, where he established a successful confectionery business. In 1870 he moved his residence and factory to the predominantly German community of Stapleton, Staten Island, where his business continued to flourish. By combining imaginative late-Victorian decorative style with appealingly sweet biscuits and confections, Mayer attracted a wide following among urban New Yorkers.

He designed and patented specialized molds and equipment from which sweet biscuits and wafers were produced and was known as the originator of the "Nabisco sugar wafer" in America. He invented the Vienna Roll, Cigaretta, Carlsbad, Champagne, Fancy Dessert, and Virginia Sugar wafers, among others. Mayer's biscuits and confections were served at Delmonico's, Sherry's, and other fine restaurants in Manhattan and throughout the metropolitan region. Despite the popularity of Mayer's products, his manufacturing establishment remained relatively small and never employed more than fifteeen workers.

In the late 1890s he moved his family residence away from the Stapleton factory, to an impressive Victorian home on Richmond Road in New Dorp, where he later began several other small manufacturing ventures. To his line of confections he added Christmas ornaments, birch beer, and a patented room humidifier. From about 1910 until shortly before his death in 1918, he also produced and marketed gilded metal "concave sign letters."

Table decorations made from Mayer's sugar wafers, ca. 1885–90.

Vienna Sugar Biscuit chromolithographed advertising handbill or box label, Gustav A. Mayer, manufacturer, Stapleton, ca. 1870–90.

INDUSTRIAL STATEN ISLAND 87

SHIPBUILDING

Staten Island Shipbuilding Company, Mariner's Harbor, photograph by W. J. Grimshaw, ca. 1920.

Souvenir program for launching of the Richmond *by the Burlee Dry Dock Company, Port Richmond, issued by the Advance Publishing Company, 1905.*

Weekly magazine for employees of the Standard Shipyard, Shooter's Island, 1918

With the growth of American naval power and the development of extensive international shipping and trade interests at the end of the nineteenth century, Staten Island's modest shipbuilding industry underwent massive expansion. Large shipyards, particularly suited for the construction and repair of metal-hulled vessels, were founded and enlarged along the Kill Van Kull, especially at Port Richmond, Mariner's Harbor, and just offshore, on Shooter's Island. Between 1900 and 1910 a number of these firms came into national prominence—among them Townsend and Downey's yard, where the imperial German yacht *Meteor III* was constructed for Kaiser Wilhelm in 1901–2. At the outbreak of the First World War shipbuilding and repair had become Staten Island's single most important and largest-employing industry.

In 1920 there were eighteen shipyards or repair plants on the island with a total work force of 6,806 people—280 office staff and 6,526 shop personnel. The 1920 production of just four of these yards included thirty-nine freight steamers, three tankers, three refrigerator ships, two freight and passenger vessels, four 1,000-ton coal barges, and two floating sectional dry docks in addition to large numbers of scows, lighters, and other small boats.

INDUSTRIAL STATEN ISLAND

LINOLEUMVILLE

Linoleum cut detail from 1927 Wild advertisement. NYPL.

American Linoleum Manufacturing Company, Linoleumville, Hurd Martin Company, Lithographers, Detroit, ca. 1910.

At the end of the Civil War, Long Neck, the marshy peninsula on the west shore of the Arthur Kill just north of the Fresh Kills, was still one of the most sparsely populated and least developed parts of Staten Island. This obscure rural area of scattered houses inhabited by the families of small-scale farmers and watermen, many of whom were descendants of early Colonial settlers, was selected in 1873 for the site of an exceptional manufacturing venture—the first linoleum factory in America.

"Linoleum"—named by its inventor, Frederick Walton, from the Latin for linseed oil, one of its principal components—was developed and patented in England in the mid-1860s. By combining pulverized or ground cork, oxidized linseed oil, and several other ingredients and rolling the mixture onto a canvas, jute, or burlap backing, an ornamental floor-covering material could be mass-produced that was flexible, durable, and comparatively inexpensive. Exported from England, Walton's Patent Linoleum Floor Cloth soon attracted the attention of American consumers and businessmen.

In 1873 Joseph Wild and Company of New York, a firm that specialized in the distribution and sale of carpets and floor coverings, secured the patent rights to the process and, with the backing of Walton's and other English capital, formed the American Linoleum Manufacturing Company. A three-hundred-acre tract on Long Neck was purchased by the company, and in less than a year a factory with docking facilities, workers' cottages, and the beginnings of a new industrial village, Linoleumville, had been created. Walton himself came to the site and supervised the construction and installation of the factory, which began operation in early 1874 with a work force largely imported from Britain. The first goods, which were sent to market in the fall of that year, were immediately successful, and the factory and its surrounding village expanded rapidly.

Noon at the American Linoleum Manufacturing Company, Linoleumville, photograph by Willard D. Decker, ca. 1900.

Unloading linseed or cork, Linoleumville, ca. 1900–10.

Factory workers at break, Linoleumville, ca. 1910. Courtesy of Percy E. Decker, Sr.

INDUSTRIAL STATEN ISLAND 93

WILD'S FOR WEAR

Under the direction of David N. Melvin (1840–1914), a Scottish-born mechanical engineer and inventor who helped construct the linoleum plant and became its supervisor after Walton's return to England in 1874, the factory pioneered in the development of improved machinery and manufacturing methods and new varieties of linoleum products. Melvin introduced variously colored, "inlaid," and "battleship" linoleum (originally made for the U.S. Navy as a splinter-free floor surface for war vessels and later gaining wide use in large office buildings, institutions, and department stores). In 1882 the Linoleumville plant employed 175 to 200 workers, utilized electric lighting to permit night-shift (in addition to daytime) manufacturing, and was producing nearly 400,000 square yards of floor covering annually. At the height of its operations between about 1905 and the late 1920s, the factory employed 700 men and women (approximately half the population of Linoleumville) and was manufacturing more linoleum in a week—90,000 square yards—than it initially produced in a year. By the mid-1920s the company was beginning to lose its market to competitors who were making less expensive products without the burlap backing. Acquired in 1928 by the Sandura-Wild Corporation, the factory was shut down completely in 1931, a short time after the residents of the village had voted to change the area's name to Travis.

Below right and opposite: Linoleum cut details from 1927 Wild advertisement. NYPL.

Advertisement for Wild's Battleship Linoleum, from Carpet & Upholstery Trade Review, *1923. NYPL.*

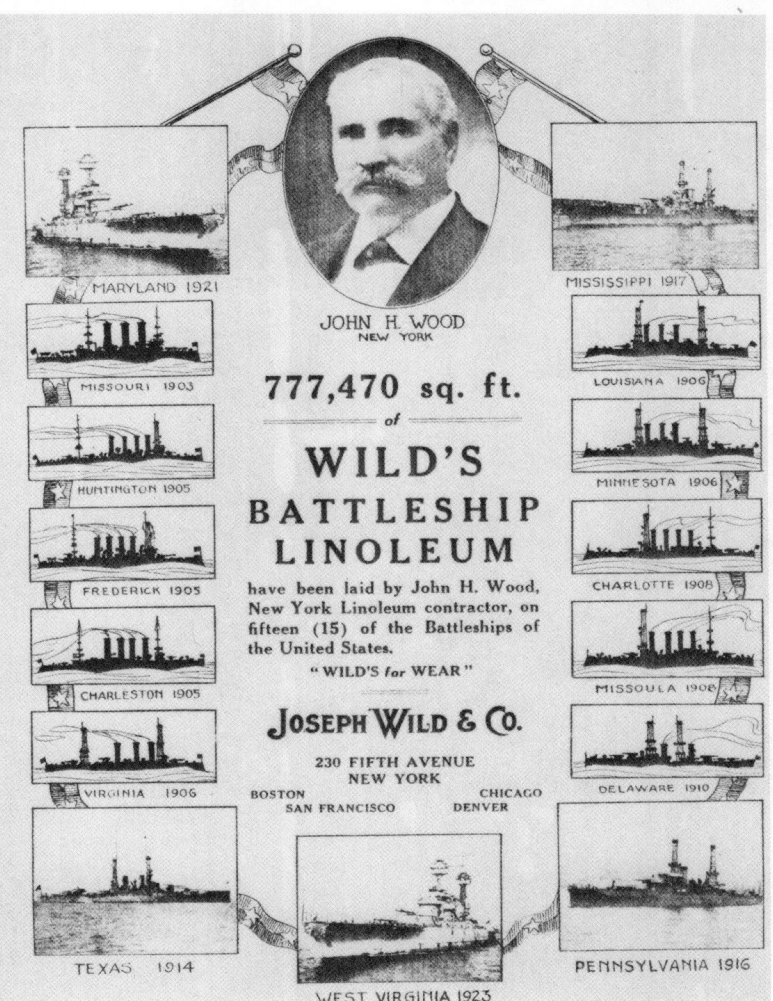

INDUSTRIAL STATEN ISLAND 95

American Linoleum Manufacturing Company employees with product samples, Linoleumville, ca. 1900.

GEZA NAGYVATHY (1866–1951)

Born in Austria-Hungary, Geza Nagyvathy emigrated to the United States with several of his brothers in 1889. First settling in Haverstraw, New York, where he found work in the brickyards, he moved in 1892 to Newark, New Jersey, residing there among a large number of other recent Hungarian and Slavic immigrants for about fifteen years and working as a shipping clerk for a firm that manufactured and imported chemicals. He married Mary Zavartkay, also of Hungarian birth, in Newark in the late 1890s and together they raised two sons.

When his employer went bankrupt about 1907, Nagyvathy moved his family to Linoleumville, where they became part of a rapidly expanding community of Hungarian and Eastern European linoleum workers. In recognition of his artistic and mechanical skills Geza was made a designer and patternmaker at the factory, a position he held until the works closed in 1931. A man of many interests, talents, and hobbies, Geza Nagyvathy wrote poetry in his native language, made and played traditional musical instruments, and devoted much time and effort to the production of elaborately hand-carved sculpture, furniture, and decorative items.

Geza Nagyvathy ca. 1938. Courtesy of Rudolph Zoltan Nagyvathy (1899–1982).

Linoleum printing roller, designed for a six-foot repeat section and carved by Geza Nagyvathy at the American Linoleum Manufacturing Company, Linoleumville, 1908.

THE GREAT DEPRESSION

WPA construction crew outside the former Richmond County Clerk's and Surrogate's Office, Richmondtown, during renovation for Historical Museum of the Staten Island Historical Society, 1934.

Abandoned buildings of the New York Anderson Pressed Brick Company, Kreischerville, 1938. Office of the Borough President, Bureau of Engineering Photographic Division.

In the national economic depression that followed the 1929 stock market crash, many of the major Staten Island employers were forced to greatly reduce operations, consolidate with other firms and relocate, or go out of business altogether. The list of Depression-era closings, bankruptcies, and factory sales includes many of the oldest and best-known establishments: Barrett, Nephews & Company Old Staten Island Dyeing Establishment; Irving Manufacturing Company's textile mill; the C. W. Hunt Company; American Linoleum; Atlantic Terra Cotta Company's Tottenville plant; and Kreischer, Anderson, and at least two other important brickworks all completely folded or moved from the island.

The tendency, already evident in the 1920s, of large regional or national corporations to absorb or merge with island companies or to establish local plants and offices continued to a limited extent during the Depression, managing to save some much-needed jobs and to create a number of new ones. Shortly before the stock market crash, J. B. King's Plaster Mills was taken over by U.S. Gypsum. Standard Varnish had been absorbed by Toch Chemicals in 1924; the Gulfport oil storage and pipeline terminal was established in 1928; and the G. Siegle pigment factory merged with the Ansbacher Corporation of Brooklyn in 1929. These examples were followed by Western Electric's important purchase of the Tottenville Copper Company, creating Nassau Smelting and Refining (1931); the construction of the Port Socony facility by Mobil Oil (1934); and the acquisition of United Shipyards by Bethlehem Steel (1938).

A small number of unemployed island craftspeople went into business for themselves. Dismissed in 1933 as chief chemist at Atlantic Terra Cotta, Walter L. Howat established a small ceramics plant near his Tottenville home.

For most Staten Islanders the only benefits from these hard times were those provided through government aid and work projects. In 1931 New York State set up the first major local relief agency in the country, the Temporary Emergency Relief Administration (TERA) in order to combat growing despair and unemployment. By March 1934 there were more than 19,000 people employed on Staten Island by various government relief agencies, about half of whom were island residents. As late as 1939, 30,000 Staten Islanders—more than one-sixth of the population—depended on relief programs for their basic necessities. Only as the defense industry began to pick up and war was declared did the dependence on state and federal government relief programs subside.

POLLUTION

Constable Hook, New Jersey, factories across the Kill Van Kull, photograph by W. J. Grimshaw, ca. 1905–15.

Protest rally ribbon, May 3, 1916. SIIAS.

The expansion of heavy industry and suburban development around the port of New York in the decades preceding the Great Depression had had a destructive effect on Staten Island's natural environment. Industrial waste and garbage disposal had become major local problems long before 1920.

Air pollution from New Jersey was a subject of concern by the early 1880s, when north shore residents organized to protest the "stench nuisance" from the Standard Oil Refinery at Constable Hook. In the early 1930s pollution-related crop damage on the truck farms remaining in the New Springville, Bulls Head, and Greenridge areas was so great that the farmers organized the Staten Island Growers' Association to lobby for pollution controls. Many truck farmers even turned to greenhouse flower cultivation to try to reduce the effects of this problem on their livelihood.

By the 1910s, the suspicion that oysters from contaminated beds were a principal cause of typhoid fever led public health and conservation officials to institute annual inspections of local waters. Jamaica Bay was condemned in 1912 and closed to oystering by court order in 1916. The Arthur Kill beds were shut down by the State Conservation Commission in 1917 but were partially reopened the next year. An epidemic of typhoid in New York City in late 1924 finally led the New York City Health Commissioner to close all oyster beds in the New York Harbor area in December of that year.

Commercial fishing—especially for the shad—had met a similar fate. Clamming, always popular but never as profitable nor as extensive as oystering, continued to be revived periodically, as the condition of local waters and clam beds permitted. Harbor and coastline pollution, particularly from industrial waste and municipal sewage systems that discharged directly into Raritan Bay, also contributed to the decline of the island's beach resorts.

The use of Staten Island as a site for New York City garbage disposal or processing has long been a subject of local concern. The construction by city officials of a garbage disposal plant on Lake's Island in the Fresh Kills in 1916–17 led to a series of violent protests by Staten Island residents. The "Garbage War" ended in 1918, when the facility was closed down by order of the Board of Health. In 1938, after much controversy, Great Kills was selected for landfill, and ten years later, the Fresh Kills marshes became the site of the world's largest sanitary land-fill operations.

WHEN YOU'RE HOT AND THIRSTY

THAT'S THE TIME YOU TAKE YOUR HAT OFF TO A GLASS OF

R. & H. BREW

"That Good Old Drink"

Rubsam & Horrmann Brewing Co.

Stapleton, Borough of Richmond
New York City

Tel. 1260 St. George

PROHIBITION AND REPEAL

Counterclockwise from top left:

R & H introduces New Crown Premium Beer with opera star Barbara Gibson (crowned), May 10, 1952, photograph by Herbert Flamm.

R & H clock tower dedication ceremony, October 12, 1936. The rebuilding and rededication of the R & H clock tower, the centerpiece and symbol of the Stapleton community, which had been destroyed by fire in 1930, attested to the vitality and importance of the brewery during the Depression. Eight thousand people attended the clock tower unveiling on October 12, 1936, part of R & H's gala celebration of its sixty-eighth birthday.

Piel's clock tower, Stapleton, 1957.

Advertisement for a Prohibition Era malt beverage called R & H Brew, from The Islander, *November 1927.*

Nebraska's ratification on January 19, 1919 of the Eighteenth Amendment to the Constitution, prohibiting the "manufacture, sale, or transportation of intoxicating liquors" brought into being a great national moral experiment that had enormous economic consequences on Staten Island. The culmination of decades of lobbying by Protestant reformers, many of whom helped found the island's temperance developments, National Prohibition, as defined by the Volstead Act of October 1919, resulted in the disappearance of all but one of the Staten Island breweries.

The Bachmann-Bechtel Company, formed about 1910 by the merger of two of the island's leading breweries, failed almost immediately. Monroe Eckstein's Manor Brewery, a much smaller enterprise, continued to operate through the 1920s, producing "near beer" until it was closed by federal agents for illegal production of alcoholic beverages. Only Rubsam and Horrmann's managed to survive the Prohibition Era and achieve renewed success in the 1930s and 1940s. By manufacturing cereal beverages with less than one-half percent alcohol by volume—R & H Brew, Tap, Malt Tonic, and others—and by converting portions of the plant to artificial ice production, R & H remained in operation through the modification of the Volstead Act in April 1933 and the ratification of the Twenty-first Amendment to the Constitution on December 5, 1933. At midnight on April 7, 1933, 3.2 percent beer was again legal in New York.

In the late 1940s and early 1950s the Rubsam and Horrmann brewing company, like many other of the city's smaller, local industries, struggled to remain competitive in a field becoming increasingly dominated by large regional and national corporations. Aggressive advertising and marketing schemes—the launching of the R & H blimp from the Staten Island Airport, New Springville, in October 1948, and the campaign to promote R & H Light and Crown Premium beers in 1952–ultimately proved unsuccessful. Plagued by labor problems, a strike, and declining sales, R & H shut down in December 1953.

The brewery was then purchased by Piel Brothers, Inc., which produced and distributed Piel's Light and Trommer's Red Letter beers from the site. In September 1962, Piel was acquired by Drewrys Limited U.S.A., Inc., Indiana. After nine years of operation, Piel closed its Staten Island plant in January 1963. In August 1976, the long-vacant R & H complex was demolished.

POST-DEPRESSION INDUSTRIES

S. S. White foundry at Prince Bay plant, Hazard Advertising photograph, 1958. Courtesy of Joseph Helmer.

Advertisement for Bosco Milk Amplifier from the Staten Island Chamber of Commerce 50th Anniversary Report, 1945.

During the 1940s, most of the island's larger industrial establishments that had survived the Great Depression continued to grow, adjusting at first to the wartime economy and then to the demands of postwar consumerism. Over the next three decades the character and significance of industrial production on Staten Island fluctuated greatly, reflecting major changes in technology, regional development, and the state of the economy.

Preparations and support for the military effort during World War II created a massive increase in industrial production and employment. The old United Drydock marine repair yard in Mariner's Harbor, acquired by Bethlehem Steel in 1938, was instantly transformed into a major manufacturer of naval vessels, with 12,000 employees (one-fifth of the available adult workforce for 1941). The S. S. White Co., U.S. Gypsum, Louis Dejonge paper works, Procter and Gamble's Port Ivory plant, and Nassau Smelting and Refining all increased production for government use and for the war effort. At the close of the war, there were 166 manufacturing firms in operation on the island, many of which had been established in the nineteenth and early twentieth centuries, employing an average of 6,080 people annually. Post-war expansion by Procter and Gamble, the Wallerstein Company (inventor of Bosco milk amplifier), Standard-Toch (formerly Standard Varnish) and other major firms, and the arrival of many small new enterprises resulted in increased industrial production and employment. By 1952 there were over 12,238 individuals employed in 252 factories on Staten Island.

During the 1950s, a number of the island's oldest and most distinctive factories began to fail. The 104-year-old Ettlinger box company and the Macrae and Rose Print Cutting Company both closed in 1958. Larger industries, such as Muralo Paint and International Fire Extinguisher, began to move their plants to New Jersey, where taxes were lower, more land was available for expansion, and modern production facilities could be built.

In the 1960s, Bethlehem Steel shut down its shipyard, the Onyx Chemical Corporation (which had acquired the International Ultramarine Works in Rossville in 1947) folded, as did several north shore textile factories. At the end of the decade and the beginning of the 1970s, high taxes and the rapidly increasing costs of energy and prospective rehabilitation, retooling, or expansion of aging, inefficient factories led many other major industries to close or move

Dreft packaging line, Procter & Gamble Manufacturing Company, Port Ivory, photograph by Herbert Flamm, 1949.

Band uniforms made by Uniforms By Ostwald, Inc., New Brighton, photograph by Herbert Flamm, ca. 1957. In 1945 Uniforms By Ostwald, Inc. moved its manufacturing operations from Manhattan to a modern plant on Richmond Terrace in New Brighton. One of the foremost businesses of its kind in the country, the Ostwald factory employed about 300 people and produced 1,500 band uniforms each week during the 1950s and 1960s. The firm had a national reputation and clientele; among its prominent customers was the West Point Band. Changing economic and social circumstances lead to a major decline in business in the 1970s. Uniforms By Ostwald, Inc. closed in 1981.

Sun Chemical laboratory, Rosebank, ca. 1960. Courtesy of Sun Chemical Corporation Pigments Division.

elsewhere. The Wallerstein Company left the island in 1971; S. S. White, acquired by Pennwalt in the late 1960s, abandoned the Factory by the Sea for New Jersey in 1972, the same year Bethlehem Steel's propeller plant closed; and one year later U.S. Gypsum moved to Port Reading, New Jersey.

In 1979 there were 118 industrial establishments on Staten Island, only nine of which employed 100 or more persons. Of the island's ten largest, non-governmental employers in 1980, only two—Procter & Gamble and Nassau Recycle Corporation—were manufacturing establishments; the others were department stores, hospitals, and health-care facilities.

Staten Island ferry under construction at Bethlehem Steel Shipyard, Mariner's Harbor, photograph by Herbert Flamm, 1951.

Nassau Recycle Corporation foundry room, Tottenville, photograph by Herbert Flamm, 1952.

ISLE OF PEACE AND PROFIT

Advertisement for "Little Farms" on Staten Island, March 1909.

Flyer for "The Isle of Peace and Profit" published by developer Cornelius G. Kolff, 1927.

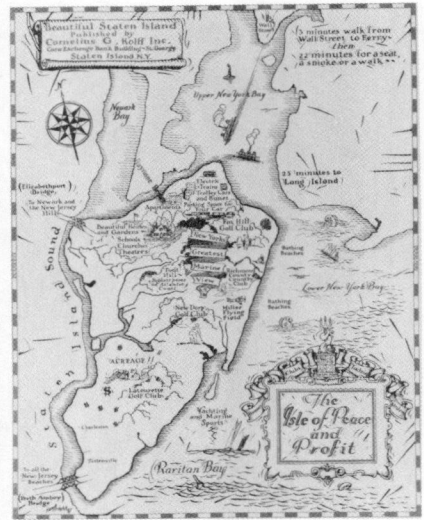

Among Staten Island's greatest resources have always been an abundance of undeveloped land and an appealing natural beauty. "God might have made a more beautiful place than Staten Island, but He didn't," wrote George William Curtis, island resident and popular nineteenth-century author—thus creating a slogan for one of the area's most successful and influential real estate brokers in the 1910s.

As the other areas of what became Metropolitan New York and the nearby New Jersey counties grew ever more urban and densely populated, Staten Island's appeal as a place for "homeseekers" and the pressure for suburban development increased. As pollution, soil depletion, and land taxes made farming less profitable, and property and income taxes and labor costs made the maintenance of large estates impractical, more island acreage became available for subdivision and residential use.

The improvements in transportation, utilities, and public services that both led up to and resulted from the island's consolidation into New York City in 1898 helped increase the number of inhabitants and create a demand for additional housing. Between 1900 and 1930 population grew by 136 percent—from 67,021 to 158,346—predominantly along the north and east shores. This represented a miniscule gain when compared to the city as a whole, which rose from 3.4 to almost 6.9 million during the same period. As one real estate broker proclaimed in the mid-1920s: "Staten Island's growth is yet to come—it is New York City's future Bronx."

To spur greater development city, borough, and, later, Port Authority officials made plans during the 1910s and 1920s to connect Staten Island to New Jersey, Brooklyn, and Manhattan by a series of vehicular bridges and subway tunnels. The Goethals Bridge, spanning the Arthur Kill between Holland Hook and Elizabeth, and the Outerbridge Crossing, connecting Richmond Valley and Perth Amboy, were both opened in 1928. The Bayonne Bridge, over the Kill Van Kull between Port Richmond and Bayonne, was completed in 1931. After years of discussion, borings for a subway tunnel under the Narrows to Brooklyn to connect with the Fourth Avenue line were actually begun in 1923, but the project was abandoned at the beginning of the Depression. Several other brief attempts were made during the early 1930s, but these too were given up in favor of a suspension bridge.

Proposed bridge over the Narrows—"This Three Quarters of a Mile of Concrete and Steel May Soon Span the Waters of Lower New York Bay"—from the Staten Island Chamber of Commerce Annual Report *for 1929.*

Program for testimonial dinner honoring Cornelius G. Kolff for activity ca. 1920–36.

Formal plans for a Narrows bridge and a connecting arterial highway system were drafted immediately after the Second World War. Final approval of the project suffered many delays, and ground was not broken until August 1959. The Verrazano-Narrows Bridge opened to traffic November 21, 1964; a second (lower) roadway was completed five years later.

As the third largest borough in area and historically the least densely populated, Staten Island has been experiencing continued growth, most dramatically in its southern and interior areas, while the rest of the city has lost population. Between 1960 and 1980 Staten Island's population rose from 221,991 to 359,442. By the early 1980s, the island was considered the fastest growing county in New York State and the leader in the construction of new housing.

Leo Sander's Meadow Brook Dairy, 100 Canal Street, Stapleton, photograph by H. Kiener, ca. 1910. At the beginning of the twentieth century, dairy farming and the processing and packaging of milk products for local consumption were still important activities on Staten Island. In 1900 there were more than eighty milk dealers, many of whom operated small farms and bottling plants in addition to providing delivery service.

Among the best known and most successful of these enterprises is the Weissglass Goldseal Dairy Corporation, which was founded in 1899 when Julius Weissglass (1873–1946), an immigrant from Austria, purchased the 50-acre Simonson farm on Watchogue Road. Raising mostly chickens at first, the Weissglass family began selling their surplus eggs and milk to other members of the Staten Island Jewish community. After a period of slow development the business expanded in the 1920s when the firm, managed by Julius' three sons, stopped raising cows on Staten Island and purchased a large creamery in Orange County. In 1933 the Weissglass Dairy opened a large milk processing and bottling plant in Mariners Harbor, which remained in operation until 1975. Since that time the business has continued from the firm's Jamaica, Queens headquarters.

112   MADE ON STATEN ISLAND

Aerial view of Staten Island farms at Bull's Head, photograph by Herbert Flamm, 1934.

Real estate brochure for "South New York" published by Wood, Harmon & Company, 1906.

ISLE OF PEACE AND PROFIT

SELECTED BIBLIOGRAPHY

One of the goals of this project was to document the industrialization of Staten Island from the early nineteenth century to the mid-1980s. Since no modern history addressed the subject in any detail, many primary and secondary sources were consulted. Research involved examination of all available federal and state census schedules and reports pertaining to Richmond County; the maps, atlases, and business and commercial directories for the island; the surveys, studies, and annual reports issued by the chamber of commerce; and the vast ephemeral literature promoting local commerce, real estate, industrial development, and tourism. The principal secondary histories of Staten Island were reviewed and abstracted and indexes to historic newspapers and periodicals at the Staten Island Historical Society and the Staten Island Institute of Arts and Sciences and the clipping and vertical files at both institutions were scanned. This effort resulted in an index card file of Staten Island businesses and industries containing more than 1,500 detailed entries that served as the framework for the Made on Staten Island exhibition and this publication. The preliminary data was augmented by findings in original manuscripts, business records, advertising and promotional materials, local newspapers and periodicals in the collections of the historical society, the Staten Island Institute of Arts and Sciences, and other libraries and archives in the metropolitan area.

The bibliography that follows is provided as reference for the text and to encourage research relating to Staten Island history. Most of the titles included are available at either the Library and Archives of the Staten Island Historical Society, the Staten Island Institute of Arts and Sciences, or at the Research Division of the New York Public Library. Essential public records may be found at the Richmond County Clerk's Office in Borough Hall, St. George. General sources are listed by type in chronological order. Especially useful periodicals, a brief list of useful manuscript and special collections, and some selected secondary sources have also been included.

I. GENERAL SOURCES:

Business, commercial, and residential directories

Richmond County Register. New York: Henry E. Tudor, September, 1862.

Handbook of the Staten Island Railroad, with Descriptive Sketches of the Villages on the Route, Names of Business Men, &c, Making a Complete and Valuable Business Directory. New York: Metropolitan Advertising Co., 1870.

The Staten Island Business Register and Railroad and Steamboat Guide (1879–1880). Bayonne, N.J.: W. E. Scudder & Co., 1879.

Webb's Consolidated Directory of the North and South Shores, Staten Island, 1882–83. New York: Webb Brothers & Co., 1882. Later editions document 1884 and 1890–91.

Slater, J. G., comp. *Webb's Consolidated Directory of the North and South Shores, Staten Island, 1892–93.* Poughkeepsie, N.Y.: A. V. Haight, 1892.

The Standard Directory of Richmond County, for the Year 1893–1894. New Brighton, N.Y.: Robert Humphrey (Richmond County Standard Press), 1893. Later editions document 1895–96 and 1897–98.

Stapleton, Tompkinsville, New Brighton, West New Brighton, Clifton and Port Richmond, Staten Island: Their Representative Business Men and Points of Interest. New York: Mercantile Publishing Co., 1893.

Industries of Staten Island Before Consolidation. New York: Richmond Publishing Co., 1898.

Trow's Business and Residential Directory of the Borough of Richmond. Vol. I. New York: Trow's Directory, Printing & Bookbinding Co., 1898. Volume II was published in 1899 and a subsequent edition followed in 1900.

Libby, Daniel P., comp. *Standard Directory of Richmond Borough (1903).* Staten Island, N.Y.: Daniel P. Libby and Charles T. Wood (Richmond Borough Publishing and Printing Co.), 1903. A later edition documents 1906.

Richmond Borough Business Directory, 1911. West New Brighton, N.Y.: A. Y. Hubbell, 1911. Later editions document 1912 and 1914.

Richmond Borough Directory, 1912. South Norwalk, Conn.: Directory Company, Publishers, 1912.

The Credit Experience Guide . . . Staten Island, N.Y. District. Pittsburgh: Merchants Mercantile Agency, 1913.

Staten Island Advance Business and Telephone Directory, 1921–1922. Staten Island: Richmond County Advance Publishing Co., 1921. A later edition documents 1922–23.

The Oleck Red Book for Staten Island, Covering the Entire Borough of Richmond, New York, Classified Telephone Directory (January 1924). New York: The Stanley Oleck Publishing Corporation, 1924. A subsequent Oleck directory documents 1928–29.

Richmond County Professionals Directory. Staten Island, N.Y.: Staten Island Chamber of Commerce, 1927.

Polk's Staten Island (Borough of Richmond) Directory for 1933–34. New York: R. L. Polk & Co., Inc., 1933.

Staten Island (Borough of Richmond) Classified Telephone Directory and Index Book, 1936. New York: Bell Directory Publishers, 1936.

Promotional literature: books and pamphlets

Edwards, Richard, ed. *A Descriptive Review of the Manufacturing and Mercantile Industries of the City of Brooklyn, and Towns of Long Island and Staten Island.* Part 2. New York: Historical Publishing Co., 1883.

Judson, S. C. *Illustrated Sketch Book of Staten Island, New York, Its Industries and Commerce.* New York: S. C. Judson, 1886.

Kobbé, Gustav. *Staten Island: A Guide Book, with Illustrations and a Road Map.* New York: Gustav Kobbé, 1890.

Prominent Men of Staten Island, 1893. New York: A. Y. Hubbell, 1893.

Reports of the Women's Committee of Richmond Co., N.Y. for the World's Columbian Exposition, 1893. New York: John Polemus, ca. 1892–93.

Staten Island Chamber of Commerce. *Staten Island, New York: Property, Commercial, Shipping, and Industrial Interests.* West New Brighton, N.Y.: Advance Steam Print, 1896.

Staten Island Chamber of Commerce Annual Report (June 1898). Other useful annual reports and descriptive statements were issued by the chamber of commerce in 1911, 1913, 1923, 1926, 1927, 1928, 1929, 1930, 1936, 1939, 1945, and 1952.

Industrial Number Descriptive of and Illustrating Staten Island, Greater N.Y., of the *American Journal of Commerce*. 2 vols. Ca. 1898 and ca.1900.

Richmond Borough: Its Real Estate, Railroads, Trolleys, Improvements and Industries—Information for Homeseekers. New York: A. V. Hubbell, 1906.

Loux, Du Bois H. *Richmond: The Busy Beautiful Island Borough of Greater New York.* West New Brighton, N.Y.: Star Publishing Co., 1913.

Richardson, Darby, comp., ed. *Staten Island, Borough of Richmond, New York City.* Saint George, N.Y.: Staten Island Chamber of Commerce, 1914.

Picturesque Staten Island and Its Prominent Citizens. Stapleton, N.Y.: Turpisch-Hampton Publishing Co., ca. 1915.

Van Name, Calvin. *Borough of Richmond's Solution of Housing Problem.* Staten Island: Office of the President of the Borough of Richmond, 1920.

Staten Island, New York City: Its Industrial Resources and Possibilities. New York: Industrial Bureau of the Merchants' Association of New York, 1922.

The Port Richmond Board of Trade. M & M Exposition. New York, 1922.

Fresh Kills Land Fill. Published by the city of New York, the Borough President of Richmond, the Construction Coordinator, the Department of Sanitation, and the Department of Parks, November 1951.

Staten Island Chamber of Commerce. *A 15-Week Study of Industrial & Civic Activities, October 2, 1952–January 29, 1953.* Staten Island, 1953.

Staten Island Chamber of Commerce. *Staten Island's Future.* Staten Island, 1957.

Staten Island Chamber of Commerce. *Staten Island . . . Rediscovered: An Area Survey by Industrial Development and Manufacturers Record.* Staten Island, October 1959.

New York City Department of Commerce and Public Events. "Manufacturing in Staten Island." *New York City Monthly Statistics* 3, no. 11 (January 1961).

Staten Island: An Industry and Economic Development Profile. New York: New York Interface Development Project, March 1982.

Staten Island Chamber of Commerce. *Statistical Guide: Staten Island, New York, 1982–1983.* Staten Island, 1983.

Staten Island Chamber of Commerce. *1983 Business/Professional Directory and Buyer's Guide.* Staten Island, ca. 1982–83.

Atlases and maps

Dripps, M. *Map of Staten Island or Richmond County.* Philadelphia: A. Kollner, 1850.

Butler, James. *Map of Staten Island or Richmond County, New York.* New York: Mayer & Co., 1853.

Walling, H. F. *Map of Staten Island, Richmond County, New York.* New York: D. A. Fox, 1859. Includes a useful business directory.

Beers, F. W. *Atlas of Staten Island, New York.* New York: J. B. Beers & Co., 1874.

Insurance Atlas of Staten Island, New York. New York: Charles L. Meyer, 1874.

Insurance Maps of Staten Island, New York. New York: Sanborn Map & Publishing Co., 1878.

Atlas of Staten Island, New York. New York: Sanborn Map & Publishing Co., 1885 (corrected 1891).

Beers, J. B. *Atlas of Staten Island, Richmond Co., New York.* New York: L. E. Neuman & Co., 1887.

Insurance Maps of the Borough of Richmond, City of New York. New York: Sanborn-Perris Map Co., 1898 (corrected up to 1911).

Atlas of the Borough of Richmond, City of New York. 2d ed. New York: E. Robinson, 1907.

Atlas of the City of New York, Borough of Richmond, Staten Island. 2 vols. Philadelphia: G. W. Bromley & Co., 1917.

Census records, statistical abstracts, and reports

Dubester, Henry J. *State Censuses: An Annotated Bibliography of Censuses of Population Taken After the Year 1790 by States and Territories of the United States.* 1948. Reprint. New York: Burt Franklin, 1969.

Coxe, Tench. *A Statement of the Arts and Manufactures of the United States of America, for the Year 1810.* Philadelphia: A. Cornman, 1814.

Spafford, Horatio Gates. *A Gazetteer of the State of New-York.* Albany: H. C. Southwick, 1813.

Digest of Accounts of Manufacturing Establishments in the United States, and of Their Manufactures. Washington, D.C.: Gales & Seaton, 1823.

Census of the State of New-York for 1835. Albany: Croswell, Van Benthuysen & Burt, 1836.

New York State Census, Richmond County. 1835, 1855, 1865, and 1875.

Gordon, Thomas F. *Gazetteer of the State of New York.* Philadelphia: P. G. Collins, 1836.

Compendium of the Enumeration of the Inhabitants and Statistics of the United States (Sixth Census), Washington, D.C.: Thomas Allen, 1841.

Barber, John W. and Henry Howe. *Historical Collections of the State of New York.* New York: S. Tuttle, 1841.

Dickenson, Richard B. *Census Occupations of Afro-American Families on Staten Island, 1840–1875.* Staten Island: Staten Island Institute of Arts and Sciences, 1981.

The Seventh Census of the United States, 1850. Washington, D.C.: Robert Armstrong, 1853.

De Bow, J. D. B. *Statistical View of the United States.* 278–83. Washington, D.C.: Beverley Tucker, Senate Printer, 1854.

United States Census, Richmond County, New York. Washington, D.C.: GPO, 1860 and 1870.

"Manufactures." Vol. 8 of *United States Census 1860.* Washington, D.C.: GPO, 1864.

French, J. H. *Gazetteer of the State of New York.* Syracuse, N.Y.: R. P. Smith, 1860.

Peters, Theodore C. *Report on the Agricultural and Other Resources of the State of New York.* Albany: Van Benthuysen's Steam Printing House, 1864.

The Statistics of the Wealth and Industry of the United States, Vol. 3. 210–13. Washington, D.C.: GPO, 1872.

"Manufactures." Vol. 2 of *United States Census 1880.* Washington, D.C.: GPO, ca. 1883–84.

"Totals for States and Industries." Part 1 of *Report on Manufacturing Industries in the United States at the Eleventh Census, 1890.* Washington, D.C.: GPO, 1895.

"Manufactures—Reports by States, with Statistics for Principal Cities." Vol. 9 of *United States Census 1910—Thirteenth Census.* Washington, D.C.: GPO, 1912.

"Manufactures, 1919." Vol. 9 of *Fourteenth Census of the United States Taken in the Year 1920.* Washington, D.C.: GPO, 1923.

United States Census Reports, Agriculture. Washington, D.C.: GPO, 1900, 1910, and 1930.

United States Census Reports, Population. Vol. 3, part 2, 282. Washington, D.C.: GPO, 1932.

New York State Conservation Commission. Annual reports for 1912, 1915, 1916, 1917, 1918, 1919, 1920, 1923, 1927.

"Richmond County." In *A Statistical Abstract Supplement: County and City Data Book, 1956.* 206–209. Washington, D.C.: GPO, 1957.

"New York Counties." Vol. 1, part 7 of *United States Census of Agriculture: 1959 Final Report.* Washington, D.C.: Bureau of the Census, 1961.

Secondary sources: local histories

Bayles, Richard M., ed. *History of Richmond County.* New York: L. E. Preston Co., 1887.

Clute, J. J. *Annals of Staten Island, From its Discovery to the Present Time.* New York: Charles Vogt, 1877.

Leng, Charles W. and William T. Davis. *Staten Island and Its People, A History: 1609–1929.* 5 vols. New York: Lewis Historical Publishing Co., 1930.

Lynd, Margaret Louise, ed. *Staten Island and Staten Islanders.* New York: Grafton Press, 1909.

Morris, Ira K. *Morris's Memorial History of Staten Island.* 2 vols. New York: Memorial Publishing Co., 1898, 1900.

Smith, Dorothy Valentine. *Staten Island: Gateway to New York.* Philadelphia: Chilton Book Co., 1970.

Staten Island: A Resource Manual for School and Community. New York: Board of Education of the City of New York, 1964.

Steinmeyer, Henry G. *Staten Island, 1524–1898.* New York: Staten Island Historical Society, 1950.

II. PERIODICALS

Numerous articles on particular industries and economic developments have appeared in the following journals for which indexes are available: *Proceedings of the Staten Island Institute of Arts and Sciences* (1908–   ) and *Staten Island Historian*, a quarterly published by the Staten Island Historical Society (1938–   ).

III. MANUSCRIPT & SPECIAL COLLECTIONS

At the Staten Island Institute of Arts and Sciences, Library and Archives: William T. Davis Collection, Notebooks and Photographs; Environmental Collection; Balthazar Kreischer Collection; Hugh Powell Collection; and Staten Island Business and Industry Collection.

At the Staten Island Historical Society, Library and Archives: Agriculture Records Collection; American Linoleum Manufacturing Company Collection; Atlantic Terra Cotta Company Collection; Brewing Industry Collection; Captain Isaac Cole Collection; Conner Family Collection; County Clerk's Office Property Map Collection; Crabtree and Wilkinson Silk Printers Collection; Cutting Family Collection; C. W. Hunt Company Collection; Cornelius G. Kolff Collection; Louis Ettlinger and Sons Company Collection; B. Kreischer and Sons/Anderson Pressed Brick Company Collection; Gustav A. Mayer Confectionery Collection; Miscellaneous Business and Industries Collection; Morgan Family Collection; Old New York Dyeing and Printing Establishment Collection; Oystering Collection; Procter and Gamble Manufacturing Company Collection; Real Estate Collection; Seaver Family Collection; Shipbuilding and Shipping Collection; Simonson Family Collection; Standring Family Collection; Staten Island Growers Association Collection; Staten Island Advance Collection; Staten Island Quartette Club Collection; John Steers Collection; U S. Gypsum/J. B. King Company Collection; Volkhardt Collection; S. S. White Dental Manufacturing Company Collection; and the Erastus Wiman Collection.

IV. SECONDARY SOURCES

Selected monographs and articles

Akerly, Samuel, M. D. "Agriculture of Richmond County," *Transactions of the New York State Agricultural Society, for 1842.* 2, 188–214. Albany: E. Mack, 1843.

———."Staten Island. Supplement to the Agriculture of Richmond County," *Transactions of the New York State Agricultural Society, for 1843,* 3, 454–461.

———.Letters on agricultural topics in *The Cultivator:* "Zea Maize or Indian Corn," in 8: 65 (1841); "Farming East and West," in 10: 50 (1843); "Ice Houses and Their Construction," in 10: 98 (1843); "Letter to Solon Robinson," in 10: 132 (1843); "Swamp Willow (Salix discolor)," in 1: 125–6 (1844); and "Swamp Willow—Basket Willow (Salix discolor—Salix viminalis.)," in 2: 126–7 (1845).

Fried, Frederick. *A Pictorial History of the Carousel.* New York: Vestal Press, 1964.

Heusser, Albert H., ed. *The History of the Silk Dyeing Industry in the United States,* 400–404. Paterson, N.J.: Silk Dyers' Association of America, 1927.

Ingersoll, Ernest. *The Oyster Industry: Tenth Census of the United States.* Washington, D.C.: GPO, 1881.

Joline, Benjamin F. *Tottenville In Retrospect.* Staten Island: privately printed, 1950.

Kochiss, John M. *Oystering from New York to Boston.* Middletown, Conn.: Wesleyan University Press for Mystic Seaport, 1974.

Olmsted, F. L., "Richmond," *Transactions of the New York State Agricultural Society, for 1850.* 10, 288–92. Albany: Charles Van Benthuysen, 1851.

"The Ornamentation of the New Subway Stations in New York." *House and Garden* 5 (February 1904): 96–99 and 5 (June 1904): 287–92.

"Polychrome Terra Cotta: Its Increased Use and Rapid Development," *The American Architect* 98 (October 26, 1910): 139–41.

Ries, Henry. *Clays of New York: Bulletin of the New York State Museum.* Albany: University of the State of New York, 1900.

Schneider, Gail. *A Cool and Pleasant Retreat But a Hungry Soil: The Clay Pit Pond Area, Staten Island, N.Y.* Staten Island: Staten Island Institute of Arts and Sciences, 1977.

Weissglass, Charles. *Smiling Over Spilt Milk, A Family History.* Staten Island: privately printed, ca. 1984.

INDEX

Page references in italics refer to illustrations.

agriculture, *112*
  dairy farming, *111*, 111
  in nineteenth century, 20–23, *21, 22, 23*
  pollution damage to, 101
  in rural economy (in nineteenth century), 17
air pollution, 101
Akerly, Samuel, 27
Allen, Clinton F., 65
American Linoleum Manufacturing Company, 90, *90, 91, 92, 93,* 96
  Nagyvathy and, 97
Ansbacher Corporation, 71, 99
Applegate, Harold, 56, *56*
Arietta Street, Tompkinsville (painting, Roche), *44*, 45
Arthur Kill, *28*
Arthur Kill Bridge (illustration, Judson), *66*
Atlantic (R & H) Brewery, 46, 46–47, *51, 102,* 103
Atlantic Terra Cotta Works (Company), *80,* 80, *81, 82,* 82, *83, 84, 85*

Bachmann-Bechtel Company, 103,
Bachmann's Brewery (Clifton), 46, *48,* 48, *50*
Barnard College (Columbia University; Manhattan), 62
Barrett, George M., 35, 36
Barrett, Col. Nathan, 40, *40*
Barrett, Tileston and Company, 36
Barrett, William, 35, 36
Barrett, Nephews and Company, 40, *40, 41,* 41
  officers of, *41*
basketmaking, 24
  by Cutting, 25
  for oysters, by Morgan, 24, 26
baskets
  by Cutting, *24*
  by Morgan, *24*
Bayonne Bridge, 109

beaches, *49,* 49, *50,* 76
Bechtel's Brewery, 46, 47
  advertisement for, *47*
Bedell, G.T., 15
  birthplace of, *14*
beer brewing, 46–47
  of bottled beer, 51
  Prohibition and, 103
beer gardens, 49–50, *50*
Bennett, W. J., *Brisk Gale in the Bay off Staten Island, A* (aquatint), *16*
Bethlehem Steel, 99, 105, 106
  Staten Island ferry constructed at, *107*
beverages, non-alcoholic, 52
Bischoff's Brewery, 46
block-cutting, 64
Book and Job Printing Shop, *45*
Bosco Milk Amplifier, *105*
bottling works, 52
Bradley, John, 21
  Mille Farm, Staten Island (painting), *21*
breweries, 46, 46–47, *47, 48, 50*
  bottled beer from, 51
  Prohibition and, 103
brick making, 60, 60–62, *61, 62, 63*
bridges, 109
  Arthur Kill, *66*
  Verrazano-Narrows, *110,* 110
Brisk Gale in the Bay off Staten Island, A (aquatint, Bennett), *16*
Brown, Philip J., 55
Brown (P.J.) Carriage Company, 55, *55*
  buggy advertisement, *54*
Bull's Head, *112*

cabinetmaking, 53
carousels, *49, 50*
carriage manufacturing, 54, *54, 55, 56, 57*
Carsten, Henry, 51
  promotion for, *51*
Carteret Shipyard, *33*
clamming, 101
clay mining, 60–62

Clifton Brewery (Bachmann's), 46, *48,* 48, *50*
Cole, Capt. Isaac, *31,* 31
Coles, James, 52
commerce
  seaboard, 31
  see also industries
Coney Island (Brooklyn), 50
confectioneries, 86, 87
Constable Hook (N. J.), *100*
Constanz Brewery (Monroe Eckstein's), 46, *48*
Corradi, N. (lithographer), *48*
Crabtree, John, 38
Crabtree and Wilkinson (firm), 38
crafts
  basketmaking, *24,* 24–26
  cabinetmaking, 53
  carriage manufacturing, 54
  during Great Depression, 99
  jewelry box making, 58
  silk printing, 38, *39*
  terra cotta production, 80, 82
  wallpaper making and block-cutting, 64, 65
Crisco Building, 72
Crocheron family, 18, *19*
Curtis, George William, 109
Cutting, Alfred, *25,* 25
  baskets by, *24*

dairy farming, *111,* 111
Decker family, *23*
Dejonge, Julius, 59
Dejonge, Louis, 59
Dejonge (Louis) & Company, 59, *59, 105*
dental manufacturing, 76–79, *77, 78, 79, 104,*
De Nyse, "Fatty," *44*
Douglas, Mrs. M. A. Baldwin, 64
Dreft packaging line, *106*
Drewrys Limited U.S.A., 103
Duff, Michael, 56
dyeworks
  Barrett, Nephews and Company's Staten Island Fancy Dyeing Establishment, 40–41, *41*

  community surrounding, 42–43, *43* (map)
  New-York Dyeing and Printing Establishment, 34, 35–37
  New York & Staten Island Dye House, 37
  silk printing by, 38, *39*

East European immigrants, 82, 97
Eckstein, Monroe, 46, 103
economy of Staten Island
  between 1790 and 1810, 15
  in 1920s, 70–71
  agriculture in, 20–23
  basketmaking in, 24–26
  carriage manufacturing in, 54
  after Civil War, 67
  Factoryville in, 35
  during Great Depression, 99
  after Great Depression, 105–106
  maritime trades in, 32–33
  in middle of nineteenth century, 44–45
  mills in, 18, *19*
  in nineteenth century, 17
  oystering in, 27–29
  as residential borough, 109
  seaboard commerce in, 31
  shipbuilding and shipyards in, 33, 88
  Verrazano-Narrows Bridge and, 110
Edwards, Richard, *Staten Island Farm Scene, A* (engraving), *20*
Egbert (J.) Farm and Cannery label, *20*
Ellis, Capt., 33
Elm Park, 60
Emerson, William, 17
employment
  in 1920s, 70
  after Civil War, 67
  in carriage manufacturing, 54
  in dental manufacturing, 76–79
  during Great Depression, 99
  in linoleum manufacturing, 94
  in shipbuilding, 88
  during World War II, 105
  after World War II, 105–106

Ettlinger, Louis, 58
Ettlinger (Louis) & Sons, 58, 58, 105
  factory sign, 58
Excelsior Company, 80

Factory Pond (Van Buskirk's Pond), 35
Factoryville (West New Brighton), 35
  community surrounding, 42–43, 43 (map)
  wallpaper factory in, 64
farming, see agriculture
ferries, 107
fishing industry, 32
  pollution and, 101
  see also oyster industry
Fountain, Capt. Henry, 42, 43
Fountain House Hotel (West New Brighton), 42, 43
French, J. H., 49
furniture-making, 53

"Garbage War" (1916–18), 101
Garibaldi, Giuseppe, 46, 48
Geib, William, 18
Geib's Tide Mill, 19
geography of Staten Island, 11
German-Americans, 45–46, 49
Goethals Bridge, 109
Goodyear, Charles, 35, 64
Granger, A. S., 68
Great Depression, 99
  industries following, 105–106
Great Kills, 101
Greenridge, 60
gristmills, 18
Gulfport oil storage and pipeline terminal, 99

Hadkins, John H., 52
Hadkins Bottling Company, 52
  advertisement for, 52
Hall, Farnham, 35
Hall, Joseph, 18
Haughwout, Nicholas, 18
Hayward, G. (painter), 37
Heal, Albert, 41
Heal, Baldwin, 41
Heal, Edwin B., 40
Heal, Joseph H., 40
Heal, Nathan M., 40
Heal, Peter, 41
Hesse (Edward) Oyster & Lunch Room, 28
Historical Museum of the Staten Island Historical Society, 12–13, 98
Hood, Andrew, 21
Horrmann, August, 46–47
  birthday certificate, 47, 47
housing, 109
  around Factoryville, 42–43
  "Little Farms," 108
Howat, Walter L., 99

Hunt (C. W.) Company, 68, 68, 69, 69
Hunt, Charles Wallace, 68–69

immigration to Staten Island, 45
  from East Europe, 82, 97
industries
  in 1810, 15
  in 1920s, 70–71
  breweries, 46, 46–47, 47, 48, 50
  cabinetmaking, 53
  carriage manufacturing, 54, 54, 55, 56, 57
  after Civil War, 67
  clay mining and brick making, 60, 60–62, 61, 62, 63
  confectionery, 86, 87
  decline of, 105–106
  dental manufacturing, 75–79, 77, 78, 79, 104
  in Factoryville, 35, 64
  during Great Depression, 99
  after Great Depression, 104, 105–106, 107
  Hunt (C. W.) Company, 68, 68, 69, 69
  jewelry box manufacturing, 58
  linoleum manufacturing, 90, 90, 91, 92, 93, 94, 94, 95, 96
  mills for, 18, 19
  non-alcoholic beverages, 52
  pollution and, 101
  print-cutting and wallpaper manufacture, 64, 64, 65, 65
  shipbuilding and shipyards, 33, 33, 88, 88, 107
  soap manufacturing, 72, 75, 106
  terra cotta production, 62, 80, 80, 81, 82, 82, 83, 84, 85
International Fire Extinguisher (firm), 105
Irving Manufacturing Company, 38, 38
"Isle of Peace and Profit, The," 2, 109

J. Simonson (schooner), 33
jewelry box manufacturing, 58
Jewett (John) and Sons, 71
Johnston, Algernon K., 76
Johnston, Melvin M., 76
Johnston, William A., 76
Jorden, H. (engraver), 15
Judson, S. C., Arthur Kill Bridge (illustration), 66

Kennedy, C. W., 41
Kill Van Kull, 100
  pollution of, 101
  shipbuilding on, 88
King, J. B., 70
King (J. B.) & Company, 70, 70–71, 99
Kolff, Cornelius G., 109, 110
  testimonial dinner program for, 110
Kreischer, Balthazar, 60
Kreischer (B.) & Sons, 61, 62, 63

labels (produce can), cover, 20, 23
Larkin, James, 52
Lawrence, Richard, 33
"Lenox Girl" (advertisement), 74
Lewis, Ellsworth, 28
  oyster boat of, 28
linoleum cut advertisements, 90, 94, 95
linoleum manufacturing, 90, 90, 91, 92, 93, 94, 94, 95, 96
  Nagyvathy's role in, 97
  printing roller, 97, 97
Linoleumville, 90, 90, 91, 92, 93, 94, 96
"Little Farms" (advertisement), 108
Long Neck, 90
Looff, Charles I. D., 50
Low, Charles, 52
Lowenstein, Benjamin, 71

Macrae and Rose Print Cutting Company, 64, 65, 105
Malden Dye House (Massachusetts), 36
Manhattan, "Oyster Row," 27–29, 29
Manor Brewery, 103
manufacturing, see industries
Mariner's Harbor, 88
maritime industry, 32
  in nineteenth century, 17
  see also shipbuilding and shipyards
Marsh, Isaac, 54
Martineau, Abraham, 28
  oyster sloop of, 28
Matthew, Alex, Oystering at Prince's Bay (painting), 30
Mayer, Gustav A., 86
Meadow Brook Dairy, 111
Melvin, David N., 94
Merrill (John I.) Oyster Barge, 27
Mersereau, Mr., 28
  oyster boat of, 28
Meucci, Antonio, 46, 48
Midland Beach, 49, 49
Midland Beach Carousel, 49, 49, 50
Midland Terminal Company, 49
Milburn, John, Capt. Henry Fountain (painting), 42
Mille, Andrew (Andre), 21
Mille Farm, Staten Island (painting, Bradley), 21, 21
Miller, Henry, 26
Milliken Brothers Structural Iron Works and Rolling Mill, 72
mills, 18, 19
Mobil Oil, 99
Morgan, James A., 24, 26, 26
Morgan, William, 26
Muralo Company, 70, 105
  advertisement for, 70

Nagyvathy, Geza, 97, 97
Nassau Recycle Corporation, 106, 107
Nassau Smelting and Refining (firm), 99, 105–106

National Lead Company, 71
Native Americans (American Indians), 24
New Crown Premium Beer, 102
New Jersey
  air pollution from, 101
  firms moving to, 106
New Springville, 24, 26
New York Anderson Pressed Brick Company, 62, 62, 99
  stock certificate of, 60
New York & Staten Island Dye House (ink and pencil, Hayward), 37
New York City, 109
New-York Dyeing and Printing Establishment, 34, 40
  collapse of, 41
  dyeworks of, 36–37
  establishment in Factoryville of, 35
  silk printing by, 38
  trade card of, 36
New York State, Temporary Emergency Relief Administration (TERA) of, 99
non-alcoholic beverages, 52

Old Mill at Richmond (painting, Winter), 19, 19
Old Staten Island Fancy Dyeing Establishment, 40–41
  advertisement for, 41
Onyx Chemical Corporation, 105
Outerbridge Crossing, 109
"Oyster Business, The," 30, 30
oyster industry, 27–29, 28, 29, 30
  Morgan's baskets for, 24, 24, 26
  in nineteenth century, 17
  pollution and, 101
  tonging, 28, 30
Oystering at Prince's Bay (painting, Matthew), 30, 30
"Oyster Row" (Manhattan), 27–29, 29

paper manufacturing, 59
Perth Amboy Terra Cotta Company, 80
Peters, Theodore C., 11
Philadelphia Museum of Art, 85
Piel Brothers, Inc., 103
  clock tower, 102
pollution, 101
  protest rally ribbon, 101
population of Staten Island
  in 1790 and 1810, 15
  between 1830 and 1860, 45
  in 1864, 11
  during twentieth century, 109
  current, 11, 110
Port Ivory, 72
  Procter & Gamble plant at, 73
  pumphouse, 72
  during World War II, 105
Port Richmond, 32
Port Richmond Board of Trade, 70
Port Socony, 99

118 MADE ON STATEN ISLAND

Prince Bay, 76
Prince's Bay, 30
Prince's Bay Beach, 76
print-cutting and wallpaper manufacture, 64, 64, 65, 65
printing industry, silk printing, 38, 39
Procter, William Cooper, 72
Procter & Gamble, 72, 73
  Dreft packaging line, 106
  "Lenox Girl" advertisement, 74
  Star Naphtha production, 75
  trademark, 74
  during and after World War II, 105–106
Prohibition, 102, 103

railroads, 45
Raritan Bay, 28, 28
Read, John, 24
Read, Sampson, 24
real estate brochure, 113
Renault, Lewis, Schooner J. Simonson of New York, Capt. Ellis, off Leghorn, Sept. 8, 1868 (painting), 33
resorts, 49, 49–50, 50
Richmond (ship), 88
Richmond County Agricultural Society, 23
  diploma from, 23
Richmond County Clerk's and Surrogate's Office (former), 98
Richmond Storage Warehouse and Van Company, 55
Richmond Wagon Works, 54
Robertson, William C. (engraver), 23
Roche, C., Arietta Street, Tompkinsville (painting), 44, 45
Rose, Johnston L., 64
Rose and Crown Tavern, 14, 15
Ross Sail Loft, 32
Rossville, 22, 24, 25
Rossville Bay, 28
Rubsam, Joseph, 46–47, 47
Rubsam and Horrmann's (R & H) Atlantic Brewery, 46, 46–47, 51
  "Calendar Girl" poster, 51
  clock tower dedication 102, 103
  parade wagon, 46
  during Prohibition, 102, 103
rural economy of Staten Island, 17
Rutan, James M., 33
Rutan, William H., 33

Sampson, Thomas, 23
  diploma awarded to, 23
Sander, Leo, 111
  Meadow Brook Diary, 111
Sandura-Wild Corporation, 94
Scheiper's (C. A.) Wagon Works, 57
Schenck, Adolph, 45
Schenck (Adolph) Book and Job Printing Shop, 45
Schmidt, August, 46

Schooner J. Simonson of New York, Capt. Ellis, off Leghorn, Sept. 8, 1868 (painting, Renault), 33
Schwiebert, John F., 54
seaboard commerce, 31
Seaver, Lawrence, 18, 19
Seaver, Patrick, 18, 19
Seguine's Point (Prince Bay), 76
seltzer, 52
shipbuilding and shipyards, 33, 33, 88, 88, 107
  during and after World War II, 105
Sieger, Karl A., 83
Siegle (G.) Corporation, 71, 99
silk printing, 38, 38, 39
slavery, 15
Smillie, James (painter), 15
Smith, Thomas B., 64
Smith, T. B. & R. (firm), 64, 65
soap manufacturing, 72, 75, 106
soda water, 52
South Beach, 49, 50
"South New York" (advertisement), 113
Standard Oil, 101
Standard Shipbuilding Corporation, 89
Standard-Toch (Standard Varnish), 105
Standard Varnish works, 67, 71, 99
  parade float, 71
Standring, Samuel, 18
Standring, Thomas, 18, 18
Stapleton, R & H clock in, 103
Star Naphtha production, 75
Staten Island Chamber of Commerce, 67
Staten Island Farm Scene, A (engraving, Edwards), 20
Staten Island ferry, 107
Staten Island Growers' Association, 101
Staten Island Historical Society, 12, 98
Staten Island Shipbuilding Company, 88
Staten Island Whaling Company, 32
  stock certificate, 32
Steers, Charles, 53
Steers, John, 53
  bill of sale of, 53
  sewing table by, 53, 53
Steers, Thomas, 53
Steidel, Leopold (painter), 47
Stuart, James, 17
Sturtevant, D. & A., 31
  receipt from, 31
Sun Chemical laboratory, 106

tariff petition, 36, 37
Temporary Emergency Relief Administration (TERA), 99
terra cotta production, 62, 80, 80, 81, 82, 82, 83, 84, 85

textile industry, 15
  dyeworks, 35–37
  Old Staten Island Fancy Dyeing Establishment, 40–41
  silk printing, 38, 38, 39
Thoreau, Henry David, 17
Tide Mill, 19
Tileston, William, 35
Toch Chemicals, 99
Tolima (schooner), 33
Tompkinsville, Arietta Street, Tompkinsville (painting, Roche), 44, 45
Tottenville, 33
  Atlantic Terra Cotta Works in, 80, 80, 81, 82, 82, 83
Tottenville Copper Company, 71, 99
Townsend and Downey (shipyard), 88
trade
  seaboard commerce, 31
  see also industries
trolleys, 49–50
truck farming, 23, 101
Tysen's, (David J.) Farm and Cannery label, 23

Unexcelled Fireworks (catalogue), 71
Uniforms by Ostwald, 106, 106
United Drydock, 105
United Shipyards, 99
United Standard, The, 89
U.S. Gypsum, 71, 99
  during and after World War II, 105–106

Van Name, Peter, 30
Verrazano-Narrows Bridge, 110, 110
Vienna Biscuits, 86, 87
Volstead Act (Prohibition; 1919), 103

Wallerstein Company, 105–106
wallpaper manufacture, 64, 64, 65, 65
Walter (Charles) & Son, 52
Walton, Frederick, 90, 94
Warnecke, Charles, 52
Weir, James, 54
Weissglass, Julius, 111
Weissglass Goldseal Dairy Corporation, 111
Westbrook, John, 64
Westervelt, Mr. and Mrs. Tompkins, 44
West New Brighton (Factoryville), 35
whaling industry, 32
White (S. S.) Dental Manufacturing Company, 76–79, 77, 78, 79, 104
  dentist's chair, 76
  during World War II, 105
  after World War II, 106

White, Samuel Stockton, 76
Whittemore, Samuel, 35
Wild, Joseph, 90
Wild (Joseph) and Company, 90
  advertisements for, 90, 94, 95
Wilkinson, James, 38
Willowbrook, mills in, 18
Winant, J. D., 25
Windsor Plaster Mills (J. B. King & Company), 70, 70–71, 99
Winter, C., Old Mill at Richmond (painting), 19
WPA construction crew, 98
Wolf, Joel, 21
Wood, Abraham C., 40
Woolworth Building (Manhattan), 81
World War II, 105–106

Zavartkay, Mary, 97

INDEX 119

Made on Staten Island
was designed by Christopher Holme
and produced by the
Publishing Center for Cultural Resources.
The Publishing Center is a nonprofit organization
founded in 1973 to help nonprofit educational
institutions and associations become
effective publishers. Its services, which
now extend to over 150 organizations
throughout the United States, are made
possible by grants from public agencies and
private foundations and corporate contributions.
The Publishing Center is located in New York City.